Nez Perce Country

ALVIN M. JOSEPHY JR.

With an introduction by
Jeremy FiveCrows

University of Nebraska Press
Lincoln and London

∞

Library of Congress Cataloging-in-
Publication Data
Josephy, Alvin M., 1915–2005.
Nez Perce country / Alvin M. Josephy
Jr. ; with an introduction by Jeremy
FiveCrows.
p. cm.
Includes index.
ISBN-13: 978-0-8032-7623-9 (pbk. : alk.
paper)
ISBN-10: 0-8032-7623-0 (pbk. : alk. paper)
1. Nex Percé Indians—History. 2. Nez
Percé Indians—Social life and customs.
3. Northwest, Pacific—History.
4. Northwest, Pacific—Social life
and customs. I. Title.
E99.N5J5855 2007
979.5004'974124—dc22
2007021252

Set in Adobe Garamond by Kim Essman.
Designed by Ashley Johnston.

Contents

List of Illustrations

Figures

Map

Introduction
I Am Of This Land

JEREMY FIVECROWS

I am of this land. Growing up on the Nez Perce reservation, I often heard this simple phrase and believe that it captures the essence of who the Nez Perce are. The rivers and valleys, mountains and forests of Nez Perce country hold my heart and connect me with my past. Living on the land where my culture was born, was almost destroyed, and is now recovering makes my history take on a much more real sense—it presents a reality impossible to capture in any way other than actual experience. For example, photographs of the Camas Prairie never capture the awe I feel when standing in that world of green camas stalks, with blue blooms stretching as far as I can see. Amid the sea of camas flowers I can see the wind turning the plants into a sea of gentle waves, and I realize that the preservation of this place is inextricably tied to the preservation of my culture, for they are one and the same. For my tribe this land is both a source of strength and its greatest responsibility. I truly am of this land.

The stories and legends of the Nez Perce, passed down from generation to generation, are the repository of our collected knowledge and wisdom. I grew up hearing stories about Coyote and other animals, learning from their mistakes and marveling at their deeds. What child wouldn't be impressed to learn about the fight between Ant and Yellowjacket, or how Coyote turned them to stone as punishment? I can still remember my amazement the first time I actually saw the basalt arch mentioned in the story, realizing that those weren't just words—I could see with my own eyes the place where the two warriors were locked in battle! The stories of my childhood not only explained the world around us but also taught us how to live.

My father's grandmother always told him never to fall asleep near a stream or a pond because Dragonfly would come by and sew his eyes shut. This simple reminder—much more effective than "be careful near the water"—is reinforced every time he sees a dragonfly.

The Nez Perce legend of how humans came into the world links the Nez Perce people to their homeland. The story begins with a monster intent on consuming every living thing on Earth. Just before the monster can finish eating every animal in the world, Coyote takes advantage of the monster's pride and arrogance and slays the beast. Coyote then cuts the monster into pieces and flings the pieces to the four corners of the world, spawning the various tribes of mankind. When the other animals point out to Coyote that he has forgotten to place any people where he killed the monster, he asks for some water. He uses the water to wash the blood from his hands and sprinkles the bloody wash water throughout the region, saying, "You may be few in number, but you will be powerful. Even though you will be few in number because I have deprived you, nevertheless you will be very, very, strong." In this way Coyote played a role in the creation of the Nimí·pu· (the people). The identity of my people lies in the ground from which we sprang; we were placed here with a special promise from Coyote himself. Near Kamiah, Idaho, visitors can still see the basalt knoll called Heart of the Monster and know that when the Nez Perce say we are of this land, we mean the very earth beneath us. Just as the dragonfly story has a deeper message, the story of Coyote slaying the monster has an important implication: humans sprang from a monster that was willing to consume the Earth, and pride and arrogance proved to be his downfall—traits still manifest in humanity. This is a message, and a warning, that is as true today as when the story was first told.

The Nez Perce connection to the land is not limited to our stories and legends. This land connection also defines our language, culture, and religion in fundamental ways. Growing up I often heard wind through the river maples combine with Nez Perce traditional songs, but it wasn't until I heard them sung along the Clearwater or Snake rivers that I realized that the drumming and singing were shaped by these particular places. The rolling hills of the Clearwater Valley, worn round over eons of time, or the surprisingly silent movement of a great river, or the rustling sound of wind through river maples all combine with our traditional songs to create the voice of this land. The strong, clear voices, the heartbeat sound of the drum, the warmth of the sun, the softness of the earth, and the smells of the *waweem* plants or Ponderosa pines harmonize into an orchestra of people and place.

The Nez Perce language, too, is a reflection of the sounds of this land. Here animals know their own names and freely tell all who will listen what those names are. The Nez Perce word for crow is impossible to spell with an English alphabet, but it can be closely approximated as "caw caw." I wouldn't expect anything different—every crow I have ever heard has told me the same thing. It should also come as no surprise, then, that as one other new animal became more common in their country, the Nez Perce assigned the name "moo." By listening to the world around them, the Nez Perce created a language that was truly the voice of the land and its creatures—indeed, many tribal people see that as their special gift back to the place that sustains them. They also see it as their duty: because the animals gave up to humans their power of speech, they expect humans to speak on their behalf.

The Nez Perce homeland stretches from the Clearwater River Basin to the Salmon River Basin, and from the Bitterroot Mountains to the Blue Mountains. It is a land of deserts and rainforests, great rivers and healing hot springs. Both the highest and lowest points in Idaho are part of Nez Perce country; such is the unique place that my people call home. Each place supports me in its own way. The vast huckleberry fields in the Craig Mountains nourish me both physically and spiritually, reminding me of the bounty the Earth provides and my dependence on her gifts. The cedar groves along the Lochsa River instill in me a feeling of holiness. These groves are home to towering old-growth cedars that reach to heaven like pillars in a cathedral; luxuriant ferns that draw the pure water as it flows in murmuring brooks through the glades; animals who have made the groves their home and casually bask in the safety of the forest. The sacredness of this place rejuvenates my soul, just as the moist, fragrant air rejuvenates my lungs.

Quite different from the rainforests of the Lochsa Valley are the arid rolling hills near Sımí·nekem—the confluence of the Snake and Clearwater rivers. These hills remind me that this place is very old. Newer, more rugged mountains are spectacular in their brash stance against the horizon, but the ancient hills of the lower Clearwater and Snake rivers suggest something more subtle, more defiant. Many of these hills have only grasses growing on them. With few trees to cover her here, the body of the Earth lies bare, revealing both her strength and her vulnerability. The smooth, sensuous connection between the Earth and the sky here feels harmonious and comforting. I often imagine these hills as my elders, hunched over from eons of life; tired, but with a singular beauty and dignity that only great age can impart. Indeed, these hills, rivers, creatures, and forests *are* elders—elders who taught and continue to teach the Nez Perce people how to live.

Finding meaning from and connecting with our past is something that makes us human. In today's world, and especially because we are a nation of immigrants, it is difficult for people to connect with their distant ancestors, particularly when those ancestors came from distant lands. Instead, people connect with their recent past in simple ways, like visiting a childhood home or returning to the town where their parents grew up. I consider myself extremely blessed to connect with my ancestors, both ancient and recent, through the common medium of the land. I marvel at being able to walk along the rivers and streams of Nez Perce country on the same paths that my ancestors used. I am awed to think of the generations of my forefathers and mothers who picked berries in the same patches that my family visits today, who fished for salmon out of the same rivers my family fishes each year, who enjoyed the lilting songs of the ancestors of the very red-winged blackbirds that sing here today. Nez Perce culture is based on a connection not only with the land but with the plants and animals, air and water. This is a connection both cherished and cultivated. Various assimilation policies sought to strain or even sever this connection. The strength of the Nez Perce culture and the

importance of the way of life instilled in us by our elders ensured that
our connection to the land survived—and thrived.

I have often heard the phrase "we are at a crossroads" being used
to describe a tribe's entrance into the modern world. I would like to
think that the Nez Perce tribe passed that crossroads long ago and today we are firmly on the path of self-determination, advancement, and
the perpetuation of our cultural heritage. The Nez Perce stories that
I grew up with told about the Nez Perce War and the greed that pre-
cipitated it. They told about Chief Joseph's plea for peace and justice,
which fell on deaf ears. They told about missionaries beating any Nez
Perce people who were overheard speaking their native language. As
recently as one generation ago, children were routinely separated from
their parents and taught that they weren't as good as white children.
My own grandfather was taught that white people are always right and
their motives are never to be questioned. The hardships, indignities,
and abuse that the Nez Perce endured didn't end with the Nez Perce
War; we continue to and perhaps will always feel their effects.

I am part of a generation of Nez Perce who are reaping the benefits of the toil, sacrifices, and work of our forefathers and mothers.
We have begun to realize the benefits of higher education, increased
wealth, and self-determination. However, the world that provides
these benefits also presents the possibility of great problems. Racial
discrimination, poverty, and alcoholism have exacted a heavy toll on
the Nez Perce people. The demoralizing effects of poverty rob too
many of our children of hope, stable homes, and opportunities. The
number of youth who have been lost to alcohol-related accidents is
frighteningly high. Many people would understand it if a group so
battered by sorrow and hardship would simply give up. Fortunately, I
am proud to say, the Nez Perce continue to strive for the betterment
of themselves and their tribe. We have learned the rules of our modern reality and take pride in the fact that learning them did not cost
us our identity, culture, or pride. In fact, therein lies our strength: by
combining our traditional teachings with modern learning, the Nez
Perce have begun to play an increasingly powerful role in shaping the
destiny of the tribe, the region, and beyond. Tribal programs that

support strong families, that foster wellness, and that promote traditional arts and crafts all play a role in the renaissance of Nez Perce culture. Exemplifying these efforts are the tribal efforts to restore the salmon, wolves, and Appaloosa horses.

Salmon are a cornerstone of Nez Perce culture, and to call the salmon a staple of the Nez Perce diet would be an understatement. Yet their steady decline has made the once-unimaginable prospect of rivers without this sacred fish into an almost unavoidable reality. Historically, a typical Nez Perce ate almost a pound of salmon every day. But salmon represented much more than a source of nutrition—the salmon shaped our society and our religion as well. From an ancient legend we learned that when the Creator was preparing to bring forth people onto the Earth, he called a grand council of all creation. From them he asked for a gift for these new creatures—a gift to help the people survive, since they would be quite helpless and require much assistance. The first to come forward was Salmon, who offered his body to feed the people. The second to come forward was Water, who promised to be the home to the salmon. In turn, everyone else gathered at the council gave the coming humans a gift. But it is significant that the first two gifts were Salmon and Water. In accordance with their sacrifices, these two receive a place of honor at traditional feasts throughout the Columbia Basin. Ceremonies always begin with a blessing on and the drinking of water, followed by a prayer of thanksgiving on and the serving of the salmon. Each time I take part in this ceremony I am reminded of the central role that salmon and water play in the health of the Nez Perce people and their culture.

Fishing for salmon is just as integral an aspect of Nez Perce culture as consuming it, and the hundreds of fishing trips I have been on with my family throughout Nez Perce country have shaped my appreciation for the land, the waters, and the salmon. These trips have always been a learning experience, from playing as a child in the pristine waters of the south fork of the Salmon River to witnessing the armed conflict between Nez Perce fishers and officers of the Idaho Fish and Game Administration over the right to fish in Rapid River. On the rivers and streams of my homeland I realized that, without question, salmon are worth risking our time, our energy, and our lives. That is why it was so troubling when the number of salmon that returned to Nez Perce country each year became fewer and fewer. Declining water quality and agricultural diversions played a role, but the full-scale conquest of the rivers brought about by the hydropower system was an obstacle that the salmon could not surmount. Between 1937 and 1974 eight major dams were built between the Pacific Ocean and Nez Perce country. By the mid-1900s the salmon numbers had dipped so low that general concern turned into outright alarm that we might lose our sacred fish. At that time the Nez Perce did not have the political voice or power to oppose the dams, and in the course of a single generation they watched as the once mighty rivers of the region were turned into a series of lakes. The builders of many of these dams tried to accommodate salmon passage, but others knowingly sacrificed the fish as a cost of development. That any such dams were built was a tragedy, but, adding insult to injury, one of these dams was built on the Nez Perce reservation itself. Dworshak Dam, near Orofino, Idaho, towers almost eight hundred feet above the valley floor; its reservoir extends over a hundred miles into areas almost untouched by the modern world. Upon seeing the completion of the dam and the destruction of the valley and the salmon run that had so many times returned to it, my grandfather, having grown up fishing for salmon on the banks of Kelly Creek and the North Fork of the Clearwater, could never bring himself to return. He could not bear to see those rivers and streams—pristine enough to drink from—devoid of salmon. While the waters above Dworshak Dam may never see salmon again, the Nez Perce are doing everything in their power to make sure that salmon return to as many of their traditional waters as they can. Once extinct in the Clearwater River Basin, coho salmon are again return annually—thanks to the efforts of the Nez Perce. The Nez Perce tribe's new fish hatchery on the banks of the Clearwater River has combined state-of-the-art science with traditional knowledge to create an environment that produces hardy salmon ready to swim to the ocean and return to the wild streams of Nez Perce country. Enormous amounts of resources are being poured into this effort, and tribal youths are joining the fight to save the salmon in incredible numbers. Every year we have more and more Nez Perce fish biologists, environmental engineers, and other scientists who are offering their minds as well as their hearts for the protection of the salmon, the water, and, ultimately, the Nez Perce way of life.

The Nez Perce Wolf Reintroduction Program, which reflects the importance that the Nez Perce people place on the land and all its inhabitants, is a success that will have far-reaching effects throughout the Pacific Northwest. To the Nez Perce people the wolf has always been a symbol of strength, hunting prowess, and power. The wolf's haunting calls were often heard in the forests of our homeland and their exploits were recounted in our stories. As the human population of Nez Perce country grew, however, the number of wolves declined, due to a combination of active eradication and simply being pushed out. By the late 1900s there were no wolves in Idaho or Oregon, but promising findings from reintroduction efforts at Yellowstone National Park have opened a window of opportunity to return the wolves to Nez Perce country. While other agencies and governments shied away from the controversy surrounding the issue, the Nez Perce, out of duty and honor to the wolf, took it upon themselves to restore this important part of the ecosystem. They proved themselves capable and dedicated to the challenge. Today the wolf population is growing and the benefits to the land are evident. Now, on clear moonlit nights in the remote wilderness lands at the heart of Nez Perce country, the resonant, soulful howls of the wolf can once more be heard as it echoes in the draws and canyons—reminding us all that they are home.

The horse is not native to Nez Perce country, but its introduction had a deep and lasting impact on the tribe. Horses did more than modify Nez Perce culture—they transformed it, becoming our symbol of freedom and wealth. We welcomed them into our lives and our villages. Nez Perce horsemen, renowned for their skill in selective breeding, created the Appaloosa, a horse that was as much a reflection of Nez Perce country as the Nez Perce themselves. From the backs of these animals the Nez Perce were able to freely travel throughout the West—from the fabled buffalo hunts on the Great Plains to the incomparable salmon fishing site at Celilo Falls and everywhere in between. I cannot imagine Nez Perce country without the Appaloosa. Thinking of them conjures up images of a trail of Appaloosas, with their signature spotted coats glistening from the effort of carrying an entire village to its summer camp along trails as old as the Nez Perce themselves; or the awesome spectacle of a herd of horses thousands strong, grazing in meadows and prairies with the morning mist still thick around their legs; or Nez Perce men hunting buffalo with their unique bighorn sheep bows specially designed for use while riding. Today the Appaloosa remains a symbol of the Nez Perce. Our tribal herds graze in fields throughout the reservation and our children learn horsemanship—carrying on this defining aspect of our culture.

After living here for thousands of years, the Nez Perce know how to live in this place, they know the stories of this place, and they are forever tied to the place where our ancestors' bones eternally rest. It is a unique land and we are a unique people. We are the Nımí·pu·, and we are of this land.

It is my hope that as you read this wonderful book—especially if you do so in conjunction with a visit to Nez Perce country—that you will catch a glimpse into the culture and lands that make us who we are and gain a greater understanding of what it means to have a sense of place. As you learn about us, our history, and our connection to our homeland, think about how you can listen to and learn from the land where you live. The message that "we are of this land" is true for everyone on the Earth. I hope that what you learn from our history and our tribe will inspire you to make that phrase meaningful in your own life. *Qeʔycıyéẃyew*. Thank you.

Editorial Note

It is quite clear that Alvin Josephy had a good ear for the Nez Perce language. While not trained as a linguist, his transcriptions are quite faithful to the original Nez Perce. Though working largely from historical documents and thus having to deal with earlier recorders who often did not hear as well as he, it is clear that Josephy worked through the names in the historical record with his Nez Perce friends, teachers, and associates. In this edition of his work we have attempted to provide International Phonetic Alphabet–compatible transcriptions of the names as footnotes where possible, using the orthography for Nez Perce developed by Haruo Aoki. In some cases we are unable to provide such a transcription without undue speculation.

Welcome to Nez Perce Country

The Nez Perce Country of northeastern Oregon, southeastern Washington, and north-central Idaho is a land steeped in America's western heritage. Once it was home only to the Nez Perce Indians, but with the passage of time other people came to this land. The flow of new inhabitants began as a trickle with Lewis and Clark's "Corps of Discovery" in 1805–1806. The trickle grew in time as others came here for a variety of reasons. First came the trappers, traders, and missionaries, and then, after a discovery of gold, the trickle became a torrent of miners, loggers, farmers, and people just seeking adventure or running from some past adventure. The different interests, goals, and aspirations of these individuals and groups blended or came into conflict here as a young nation, the United States, expanded westward in the nineteenth century.

Today Nez Perce National Historical Park in north-central Idaho commemorates these people and their history. The park is like the story itself—a complex mosaic. Authorized by Congress in 1965 and expanded in 1992, it comprises thirty-eight sites—nine administered by the National Park Service and twenty-nine managed by state, tribal, local, or other federal agencies. The sites, like beads on a loosely strung necklace, are found throughout an area covering some 31,200 square kilometers (12,000 square miles). The thread linking these sites together is the history of the Nez Perce people, a people aware of their past, proud of their culture, and an active part of the present.

Whether you are traveling through this beautiful land in your automobile or vicariously in your armchair, both the Nez Perce and the National Park Service welcome you to Nez Perce Country.

Nez Perce Country

Chapter One
Before the White Man

In the beginning, before the coming of the *letí·telíwit* (human beings), the world, according to the legends of the Nez Perce people, was inhabited by animals that were endowed with the qualities of humans and behaved like them. In that mythical age, the principal character was Coyote, a trickster and transformer. At times Coyote was a silly rascal who got himself into ludicrous scrapes. At other times he was super-human and able to change himself and others, as well as the forces of nature, into different forms and to accomplish wondrous deeds.

One day Coyote learned that all the animals were being devoured by a fearsome monster who dwelled near present-day Kamiah on the Clearwater River. Tricking the monster into swallowing him, Coyote started a fire inside the monster's belly and slew him by severing his heart from his body with stone knives, setting free the imprisoned animals. Carving the dead monster's body into pieces, Coyote flung them throughout the land where they became the different Indian tribes of today. But he had forgotten the region in which the monster had lived. When Fox reminded him of his oversight, Coyote sprinkled that part of the country with the monster's blood, and from it sprang the brave and intelligent Nimí·pu· (the people). Today they are also known as the Nez Perce Indians, and southeast of Kamiah, in the center of their country, one can still see the mounds of the heart and liver of the slain Monster.

This tale is part of a huge and rich treasury of legends that countless generations of Nez Perce grandparents and parents have told their children to instruct and educate them in the backgrounds, cultural ways of life, and codes of conduct of their people. The legends convey moral teaching and practical information about familiar things and deal generally with notable landmarks of the Nez Perce terrain, the storms and winds of the mountains, the rattlesnakes among the basalt rocks in the canyons, the flowing streams and the salmon that come in the spring and summer, the insects, birds, animals, and trees, and, indeed, with all creation. In effect, the legends have not only bound together the families more tightly from one generation to the next but helped to maintain and strengthen the deep spiritual ties that join the Nez Perce people to the rugged and inspiringly beautiful part of the North American continent that is their homeland.

Nez Perce Country lies within what anthropologists have called the Plateau cultural area of the Northwest, a large inland region from the Rockies to the Cascade Mountains and from the great bend of the Fraser River in British Columbia in the north to the edge of the Great Basin in southern Oregon and Idaho. Within that Plateau area, sharing many of the Nez Perce cultural traits and lifeways, are numerous other tribes. They include to the north and northeast such Salish-speaking peoples as the Coeur d'Alenes, Spokans, and Flatheads and to the west and northwest the Wallawallas, Palouses, Umatillas, and Yakamas—who with the Nez Perce spoke closely related Sahaptian tongues of the Penutian language family—as well as Cayuses and Molalas whose somewhat different languages also stemmed from the Penutian stock.

At its greatest extent, before the coming of the white men, the territory of the Nez Perce is estimated to have covered approximately 70,200 square kilometers (27,000 square miles), extending from the eastern slopes of the Bitterroot Mountains on the present Montana-Idaho border across almost all of the southern half of Idaho's panhandle, from the area of the Palouse River in the north to the Payette River in the south, and westward across a large part of what are now southeastern Washington and northeastern Oregon. Falling within two major physiographic provinces, the Northern Rocky Mountains in most of northern Idaho and the Columbia Plateau in the west, it is a spectacularly majestic country of vast, and often abruptly changing, differences in elevation. The terrain encompasses a mosaic of forested mountains, some with elevations above 3,048 meters (10,000 feet); high plateau prairies and huge, undulating hills; steep, grassy ridges and escarpments of rimrock; and awesomely deep valleys and canyons that, in the area of Lewiston, Idaho, descend to as low as 229 meters (750 feet) above sea level.

In this breathtaking up-and-down country, temperature and climate vary as greatly as the terrain does, providing a rich seasonal variety of flora and fauna at the different elevations and on differently facing slopes. It has been said that a person can experience summer heat in the depths of a canyon, while partway up cool breezes blow and at the top snow will be falling. Although rainfall is generally about one-third that of the coastal areas west of the Cascades and summer precipitation is often sparse in the lower country, the rain and the heavy upland winter snowfalls provide adequate moisture for the development of some of the nation's most lush natural grasslands, the sustenance, in turn, of large numbers of deer, elk, and other animals. At the same time, high drainage basins have produced many cold, fast-running rivers, filled—especially in aboriginal times—with salmon and other fish. Flowing through the deep, sheltered valleys in the original Nez Perce territory, they include the Clearwater, Grande Ronde, Imnaha, Salmon, and Snake rivers, the last one world-famous for the chasm of Hells Canyon, the deepest gorge (2,400 meters or 7,900 feet) in North America. The canyon, once a part of the Nez Perce homeland, is now the border between Idaho and Oregon and the principal feature of Hells Canyon National Recreation Area.

The Nimí·pu· have occupied this "big" country of uniquely diverse topography for many millennia. Sustained archeological work in this part of the Northwest began only in the 1950s, and great gaps in knowledge of the prehistoric past still exist, with much still to be learned about the development of the Nez Perce culture. A recent work, a valuable synthesis by Kenneth Ames of Boise State University of what is known so far, makes it clear that people of a big-game-hunting cultural tradition who existed on both sides of the Rocky Mountains were in all zones of Nez Perce Country—the canyons, plateau, and mountains—at least ten or eleven thousand years ago. Evidence of their presence has been found at several archeologically explored sites, particularly at Hatwai and Lenore in the lower Clearwater Valley above Lewiston, and on the higher reaches of the Clearwater's North Fork. Whether they, or others, were there still earlier is not yet known. A series of Ice Age floods that poured through some of the river canyons and ended about thirteen thousand years ago would have scoured away any evidence that lay in the river paths, and so far no finds have been made in the high country that would push back the period of known habitation.

It is thought that these earliest nomadic small-group and family units used stemmed lanceolate spearpoints to hunt mammoths and other outsized Ice Age animals, and fished, and gathered mussels and certain berries and wild-growing foods. They have been linked culturally with other big-game-hunting peoples whose relics have been found elsewhere in the interior Northwest and who had attained a stage of development known to some archeologists as the Windust Phase. Their population in the Nez Perce area was relatively small, and evidence to date suggests that they were most numerous along the middle and lower Clearwater River.

Throughout the millennia that followed the region experienced a series of gradual changes in climate. Beginning about nine thousand years ago, that section of the Northwest that had been free of the Ice Age glaciers but had been cooler and wetter than today began to warm and become drier. As time went on, until about 2500 BC, the population grew gradually, and hunting, fishing, and gathering activities increased. It was generally a stable era, with few known important changes in material traits except for the making of more sophisticated and efficient stone implements and tools and the introduction, about 4700 BC, of large side-notched hunting points. People lived in recesses in canyon walls and other rock formations, or camped in the open, usually along a stream. If they built shelters, they were temporary ones and left no trace. Little is yet known of their diet, though it is assumed that they hunted large and small animals, particularly deer, elk, pronghorn, rabbit, and beaver, gathered freshwater mussels, and caught and ate salmon and steelhead. Gradually, they made more use of grasses and wild plants. Stone manos and metates that were used to grind seeds from wild plants during the Late Cascade Phase have been found at Weis Rockshelter in Graves Creek Canyon south of Cottonwood, Idaho; this cliff shelter has revealed evidence of almost continuous human occupation from 5500 BC to 1400 AD.

It is assumed that by the end of the Cascade stage of development some of the foundations of the historic Plateau culture, including that of the Nez Perce people, were becoming established, with minor variations being devised and adopted by different local groups. The development of the Nez Perce culture certainly quickened and broadened during the Tucannon Phase, which began about forty-five hundred years ago and lasted for some two thousand years. For the first time, evidence of this period shows the establishment of Nez Perce winter villages of circular, oval, and rectangular semi-subterranean pit houses, particularly along the lower Clearwater River. Eventually, the villages grew larger and more numerous, with individual structures as wide as 7 meters (24 feet) in diameter and containing inside circular earthen benches around deeper inner pits. None of the aboveground portions of the buildings have survived; they probably were made of pole frames covered with brush, bark, or mats.

The diet included deer, elk, antelope, mountain goat, small mammals, and birds, as well as many kinds of fish, roots, and wild-growing foods. The presence of an increasing number of stone mortars and pestles, which were used to crush roots, suggests a sharp rise in their gathering and use of roots. Why this happened is not entirely clear. During this period the climate of much of the Plateau area, including the southeastern part where the Nez Perce ancestors lived, was becoming hotter and more arid. Many people, it is suspected, were moving to, or spending more time along streams or in the cooler and moister climate of the higher country and relying more on roots than seeds.

By about 500 BC, there were numerous villages of Nez Perce ancestral groups in various parts of the southeastern Plateau. Most of the settlements were small, containing from one to three structures. It appears that the people had intensified the hunting and use of bison, which are usually associated with the Great Plains east of the Rockies but which seem to have been present in large numbers in the Columbia Plateau at least until the 1770s and in northern Great Basin areas until the end of the eighteenth century. Hunters, in the days before they had the horse, went after the bison on foot, creeping up stealthily on individual animals and probably joining in bands or intertribal groups that surrounded numbers of bison or stampeded them over bluffs and cliffs to their deaths.

On the whole, relatively little is yet known of how the Nez Perce culture developed until the last few hundred years. After 500 BC, improvements in technologies and equipment permitted a greater utilization of the rich seasonal food supplies and led to a continued growth of population. In the thousand years prior to 1700 AD, the greater numbers of people living in an increasing number of villages along the main streams and tributaries of the Clearwater, Salmon, Snake, and other major rivers intensified their use of salmon and other fish. With improved fishing gear and methods, in fact, fish eventually constituted at least 50 percent of the diet and the bounteous fish supply supported the growing population.

Obviously many questions remain about the origins of the Nez Perce. The more recent prehistoric past, however, is a different story. As a result of the oral history and individual and collective memories of the Nez Perce peoples themselves, as well as the studies of anthropologists, ethnologists, and archeologists, much more is now known about the Nez Perce and their culture in the last centuries before white men affected their lives and homeland.

It is estimated that by 1700 AD the Nez Perce population had risen to more than 4,500 and the number of permanent villages to more than 125. Comprised of extended families who were often related to each other, the population of individual villages ranged from 30 to 200, though the average may have contained about 35 inhabitants and only a few had more than 100.

The Nez Perce villages were democratic and egalitarian and possessed a relatively simple social and governing structure that recognized the freedom and equality of the people. The basic social and economic unit in each village was the family. Through marriages many families had relatives in other villages and even in certain other tribes.

In each village, the people chose a council that named and advised a headman. Often that position was hereditary, but the council could substitute an abler man for an ineffectual son of a previous headman. Sometimes the headman was also a shaman, or religious leader, possessing strong spiritual powers. Also of importance, however, were such characteristics and qualities as his wisdom, reputation for generosity, abilities at diplomacy and oratory, bravery, experience, and age. Frequently he was the village's oldest capable man. His duties were to arbitrate disputes, act as spokesman, oversee the well-being of the villagers, and provide an example of outstanding and generous conduct, sharing his wealth with the needy. In return, the people often gave him food, clothing, and other goods, especially for settling arguments. Occasionally he was assisted by prominent younger men, and through marriage ties he sometimes became the headman of two villages.

Although he was the most influential person in a village, he could not overrule the council. That body, which included the male heads of the families and sometimes other elderly prominent males, was a deliberative one that discussed village issues and made decisions only by general agreement. It planned the details of fishing, gathering, hunting, and other village activities, decided on relations with other groups, and took steps necessary to preserve the people's peace, welfare, and harmony. Women took little or no part in council discussions, but they were often able to influence male relatives on the council.

The council's authority, like that of the headman, was strictly limited. Neither could enforce compliance with their decisions. Both ruled by persuasion and influence, and dissenters within a village were free to go their own way. But their respect for the headman and council, and agreement that the decisions were necessary or good for the people, usually kept them from doing so. Those guilty of conduct that offended or harmed a village, or of a serious crime, were generally punished by relatives or, in some cases, banished from the village by the council.

Some villages ranged along the rivers in clusters, and some were widely separated. Each village was independent, but those along the same stream or in the same general locality were united in bands and were identified by name with the principal village, the stream, or the locality. Representatives of the different villages composed a band council, which elected a band leader, usually the headman of the largest village or the ablest male in the band. Generally, that office, too, was hereditary, but the council could make another selection. The bands unified the villages for group undertakings, including the building and maintenance of facilities at fishing stations, food-collecting trips, and seasonal ceremonies, as well as for mutual defense and attacks against enemies.

For much the same purposes, various neighboring bands were unified, in turn, into bigger regional groups, sometimes called confederacies or composite bands, with overall leaders selected by councils made up of the headmen of the member bands, as well as prominent warriors. The headman of a composite band was usually a man of outstanding prestige and abilities, often in hunting or warfare. The largest such group was composed of many of the bands on the upper Clearwater River, centered around the Kamiah Valley. Other major composite bands included those about present-day Lapwai; at the mouth of the Grande Ronde River; the confluence of the Clearwater and Snake rivers at present-day Lewiston and Clarkston; the Wallowa Valley and the Imnaha River in Oregon; and in the vicinity of present-day Whitebird along the Salmon River.

The composite band—important in understanding later Nez Perce history—was as high as political unification went among the villages. The people as a whole comprised an ethnic entity because of cultural and linguistic similarities, a common background, and blood and marital interrelationships. But there was no head chief, permanent council, or political organization that could speak for all of them, and even the leaders of the bands and composite groups could not force individual members to go along with the majority. Though unity on important matters was often achieved, the autonomy of each village and of each band was paramount.

Early white visitors to the Nez Perce thought they detected another, higher grouping of the villages and bands into two overall divisions and called many of the northerly people in the watershed of the Clearwater, who lived closer to the western plains and often traveled to them to hunt buffalo, the Upper Nez Perce, and the others, who were more remote from the plains and went less frequently, the Lower Nez Perce. It is believed today that this was merely a subcultural distinction between bands that spoke slightly different dialects of the Nez Perce language and showed somewhat different degrees of orientation to the plains way of living.

At the same time, the whites noticed the presence among many Nez Perce of a war chief, an outstanding hunting and war leader, as well as the headman, or, as they termed him, the peace chief. Both of them were accompanied by criers, who announced their statements and decisions to the people. It is not known when war leaders and criers first came into existence among the Nez Perce, or whether they were of Nez Perce or Plains Indian origin. By the time the whites appeared in Nez Perce Country, however, the war chief was an established figure. A man of proven prowess and skill, he was elected by the council, of which he was often a member, to conduct hunting or war parties. During those undertakings, he was the supreme authority, but after they were over, he became again subordinate to the headman, or civil leader. In a number of instances, however, the same man filled both positions, especially on the composite band level.

The riverine villages, nestled in narrow valleys beneath high hills that provided warmth, were mostly winter residences. The people lived in lodges and double lean-tos, semi-subterranean longhouses covered with mats of reeds and grasses. The longhouses, a few of which were up to 30.5 meters (100 feet) in length, housed a number of families and sometimes the entire village membership. The fires of individual families were placed in rows down the center, with the smoke going up through an opening at the ridgepole. The people slept along the inner walls of the structure. Villages also contained menstrual huts set apart from the other buildings; small, dome-shaped sweathouses used by both sexes for physical and spiritual purification and cleansing; and semi-subterranean dormitories, which sometimes also were used for sweat baths. In other seasons, when the villagers moved to fishing, gathering, and hunting camps or various interband or intertribal meeting places, they dwelled in temporary, tipi-like shelters, usually covered with portable woven mats of bark or reeds.

By the eighteenth century, garments were being fashioned from the dressed hides and furs of many animals, particularly mountain sheep, deer, and elk, but also antelope, mountain goat, bison, wolf, bear, coyote, and smaller creatures. When game was scarce, shredded bark and grasses were used. What was worn depended on the season, the occasion, and the availability of materials. Clothing included breechcloths, double aprons, leggings, poncho shirts, belts, robes and blankets, moccasins, mittens, neckpieces, and occasionally fur or animal-head caps for men and belted dresses, long shirts, skirts, aprons, leggings, poncho shirts, blankets, knee-length moccasins, and mittens for women. Women also wore fez-shaped hats of twined grasses and hemp cordage, and both sexes wore fur strips in their braided hair. Young children wore little or no clothing in warm weather, and babies were carried in wooden cradleboards to which were usually attached charms and a small bag containing the infant's umbilical cord, the destruction of which, it was believed, would bring bad luck.

Daily dress was mostly unornamented, but for special occasions people donned clothes decorated with polished elk's teeth, beads and discs of stone, bone, or shell (the last was traded inland by coastal Indians), dyed or natural-color porcupine quills, feathers, beaver teeth, paint, or other materials. In addition, sashes, bracelets, neckpieces, and other decorative accessories were made from ermine and otter skins, bear, eagle, and badger claws, pieces of fur, animal teeth, shells, bones, and other objects.

As is made clear in a study of Nez Perce dress by anthropologist Stephen Shawley, the Nez Perce appreciated beauty and cleanliness and took great care with every detail of dress. Ornamentation usu-

ally was meant to please both the wearer and observer and be an expression of one's identity, special status, or rank. "Medicine" objects
provided protection to the wearer or symbolized a personal story or
the spiritual source of one's power. Headmen, shamans, and warriors
often added extra details to denote their status.

Both sexes commonly painted their faces and bodies as protection against the sun, cold weather, and insects, but also to appeal to
the opposite sex, to be traditionally proper, to communicate their
mood or intent, or for curative and spiritual purposes. Paints were
made from minerals, clays, and ochres mixed with fish oil, mud, or
the tallow of bear, elk, and other animals and were carried in special
skin pouches that also held brushes and applicators, combs, personal
ornaments, and tweezers with which to pluck out unwanted facial
and body hairs. Both sexes also pierced their ears and wore earbobs,
pendants, beads, and strings of shells and bones in them. According
to Lewis and Clark and other early white visitors to the Northwest,
some of the Nez Perce wore a decorative dentalium shell through the
pierced septum of their nose. The practice, which was more common
among people in the upper Plateau and along the lower Columbia
River, was responsible for French-Canadian fur trappers bestowing
on all the tribal members in the early nineteenth century their historic name, Nez Perce, or pierced nose. The practice is not confirmed
by oral tradition. If practiced, it soon died out.

The aboriginal Nez Perce practiced no agriculture, and much of
their existence was occupied in seasonal food-collecting activities. In
late May and early June, the rivers filled with eels, steelhead, and chinook salmon. The villagers crowded to communal fishing sites where
they had built weirs of brush and poles to trap the fish, or rock and
wood platforms from which the men and boys could haul in fish with
large dip nets. Spears, harpoons, seines, hooks and lines, and dugout
canoes also were employed to bring in the fish that were fighting
their way upstream from the coast to spawn. The first fishing of the
season was accompanied by prescribed rituals and a ceremonial feast
known as ké⁷uyıt. Thanksgiving was offered to the Creator and to the
fish for having returned and given themselves to the people as food.

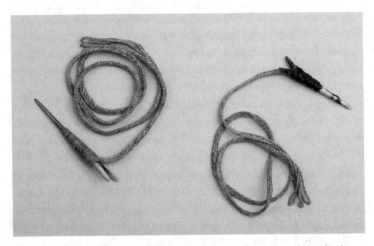

Fish made up a large part of the Nez Perce diet, for the streams abounded with salmon, trout, sturgeon, and other varieties. One of the ways the Nez Perce caught fish was with spear points and line. Courtesy National Park Service, Nez Perce National Historical Park; NEPE-HI-8774, -8775.

In this way, it was hoped that the fish would return the next year. The catches were divided among the people by shamans or specially-designated individuals, and what fish were not eaten were split open, cleaned, and smoked or dried in the sun to be stored for trade or later use. Fishing took place throughout the summer and fall, first on the lower streams and then on the higher tributaries, and catches also included blueback salmon, sturgeon, whitefish, suckers, and varieties of trout. Most of the supplies for winter use came from a second run in the fall, when large numbers of sockeye, silver, and dog salmon appeared in the rivers.

Kouse and other early root crops were gathered during the spring while the people were still along the lower streams. But after the snow melted in the higher country, the bands left their riverine villages and, with dogs helping to carry the baggage, traveled to favorite root-gathering grounds on the plateau, like Musselshell and Moscow meadows and the Weippe and Camas prairies, where they established camps.

With the people again observing "first fruits" thanksgiving ceremonies and feasts, the women used crutch-shaped digging sticks and turned up a succession of ripened roots, including camas and bitterroots. They were used in a variety of ways: eaten raw, steamed, boiled into a mush, pounded into a gruel, or shaped as dough into small cakes to be stored in hemp baskets in pits lined with grass or bark.

During the warm months, there were also wild plants, berries, pine nuts, and sunflower seeds to be gathered. In the meadows of the foothills were wild onions, carrots, and other plants, and among the underbrush of the plateau draws and forested mountainsides were hawthorn and serviceberries, chokecherries, thornberries, blackberries, and huckleberries. The berries were carried back to the camps in large containers of coiled basketry to be pressed into cakes and used later to flavor dried fish, roots, and meat.

The camps were lively communal meeting places for the different bands, each of which set up at a separate site. While the women gathered roots and berries, the men and boys hunted, fished, played games, or competed in wrestling or foot-racing. Relatives visited each other's camps and made new friendships. In the evenings, and often lasting well into the night, there were interband rituals and feasts, gambling at the stick and other guessing games, celebration dances, drumming and singing, and courting. Food was prepared by being ground with stone pestles and mortars of wood, stone, or basketry and baked in earthen ovens, boiled with hot rocks in watertight baskets, or broiled on sticks or wooden frames inserted into the ground around fires. Spoons, bowls, and drinking cups were made of wood or the horn of a mountain sheep. Other utensils and tools, such as knives, wedges, axes, scrapers, and clubs, were fashioned from antler, bone, stone, and wood. Hemp was used for flat wallets or pouches. Later, these distinctive Nez Perce bags, decorated with colored geometric designs, would be woven from corn husks.

Game animals and birds provided, besides food, material for dress, implements, and other objects of daily life, so hunting went on almost constantly except at the height of salmon runs. The principal big game included deer, elk, mountain sheep and goat, moose, bison, antelope, and brown, black, and grizzly bear. Birds included grouse, sage hens, ducks, and geese. Hunters usually went out in the predawn hours, before the animals bedded down, and stalked deer and elk at the salt licks, watering places, and along game trails that led to them. Decoys and scarecrows were used, as were nets and nooses for birds and smaller game and deadfalls for larger animals. Stratagems for flushing the game included large communal encirclement drives, and some of them were assisted by firing the grass. Other types of drives headed the game over cliffs, into prepared traps, or, by the rolling of rocks, downhill toward a waiting hunter or into a stream where men in canoes killed the animals. Men also stalked game from tree to tree, set ambushes, or, wearing antlers and skins, crept up on unsuspecting quarry. Until the bison disappeared from the area, probably from overhunting, in about 1770, they were killed in the Palouse country and on the Columbia plains on the northern and western fringes of the Nez Perce territory. Nez Perce hunted them also on the northern Great Plains, as well as in southeastern Oregon and on the Snake River plains of southern Idaho until the herds disappeared from there, too, sometime before 1845.

Spears, bows and arrows, and other weapons were used in the hunts. The bows were usually made of yew, syringa, cherrywood, or thornbush, backed by sinew, but, until mountain sheep became scarce in their country in the early nineteenth century, the strongest bows were made from that animal's horns, which were straightened by being boiled or heated and backed with layers of sinew. Other tribes, on the plains and elsewhere, admired these bows and were often anxious to trade the Nez Perce for them. Arrows were sometimes tipped with rattlesnake venom, and in the winter, hunters used snowshoes. Hunts were frequently long and unsuccessful, and men took along rations of dried meat, camas, and other roots, including one known as *tolapqat tólapqat* whose special qualities gave them strength and alertness.

Much of the food was stored against winter starving times, which were frequently serious. The villagers stretched supplies but sometimes ran out of them before spring and had to forage for anything edible, including moss and the inner bark of pine trees, which they roasted or made into a mush or soup. Sharing was mandatory, not only within a village, but among bands and even members of other tribes. Stinginess was a vice and, as was customary among peoples throughout the Plateau area, guests were treated hospitably and were even permitted to share the use of fishing stations and gathering and hunting grounds. Such mutual exploitation of economic resources was a hallmark of Plateau cultural life.

The Nez Perce not only visited frequently and intermarried among themselves but traveled widely and had social and economic relationships with many different tribes. In the spring, before the salmon reached them, Nez Perce often went down the Snake and Columbia rivers to the rapids at Celilo Falls and the Dalles, where the fish had already arrived from the coast. This was the home territory of Wishrams, Wascos, and other peoples, but the area also teemed with additional groups that had come to fish from elsewhere in the Northwest, including Wallawallas, Yakamas, Umatillas, Klikitats, Wanapums, Palouses, and Cayuses, all of whom, like the Nez Perce, spoke Sahaptian tongues. The Nez Perce were closely related by marriage with many of the Palouses and Cayuses, who lived immediately to their north and west, but they socialized, fished, and traded with all the different groups and had relatives among a number of them. Some Nez Perce also went to the Willamette Falls in western Oregon to fish and trade and apparently even traveled on occasion to the coast and far south into California.

Closer to home, Nez Perce bands journeyed to annual intertribal trade gatherings at such places as the Yakima Valley, the confluence of the Snake and Columbia rivers, and the area of present-day Moscow, Idaho. Farther north, they fished at Spokane and Kettle Falls and visited with Spokans, Coeur d'Alenes, Colvilles, and Kalispels. In the spring, when the snows had gone, large parties also crossed the mountains to the east, joining Flatheads and Kutenais in buffalo hunts on the northern plains. The Nez Perce took several routes across the mountains, including the Lolo Trail, which began at Weippe Prairie, and a southern one that took off from the South Fork of the Clearwater River. Still other hunting and trade trips were made to southeastern Oregon and southern Idaho, the territories of Northern Paiutes, Western Shoshonis, and Bannocks, who frequently traded and socialized with the Nez Perce bands at such places as New Meadows in Idaho and the vicinity of present-day Baker in eastern Oregon.

The relationships were not always peaceful. In the north, Nez Perce sometimes feuded with Spokans or Coeur d'Alenes over real or imagined insults and rivalries, and on the plains intertribal hunting groups of Nez Perce, Flatheads, and Kutenais clashed with Blackfeet from Canada. In the south, warfare with the Shoshonis, Bannocks, and Paiutes was so frequent that peaceful trade meetings with them were little more than truces. Raiding parties of the southern tribes often struck at Nez Perce and Cayuse villages, and those two peoples, frequently in allied war parties, retaliated. The Nez Perce called their southern foes the *tiwélqe*, meaning "an enemy to be fought." Raids were brief, but sometimes bloody. Some people would be slain, and others taken captive. The latter were brought back to villages and either killed or adopted as inferiors and slaves. Slaves, however, also were acquired by peaceful trade. They did menial tasks and had no voice in village affairs, but generally they were cared for like relatives, and a few became influential. Their children were not regarded as slaves.

The Nez Perce were family oriented and were raised, educated, and influenced by close relatives. Before giving birth, an expectant mother was instructed and helped by elder female relatives, who also assisted a midwife or a shamaness, as well as the girl's mother, when the baby was born. After children were weaned, they usually were cared for by their grandparents, who taught them the basic arts and skills of the people and spent long winter hours telling them myths like those of Coyote's Fishnet and Ant and Yellowjacket. The myths, about creatures that were turned to stone for their misbehavior, entertained and instructed the children in Nez Perce customs and values. They generally emphasized themes of proper conduct and attitude, including bravery, justice, generosity, repression of emotions, self-discipline and self-reliance, individual freedom, opposition to centralized authority, and dependence on supernatural forces to determine one's destiny—all of them values that would be reemphasized all their lives in their upbringing, in rituals, and by the exhortations of their leaders.

Later, children were trained also by uncles and aunts, whom they called by the same words they used for father and mother. Young children rarely were disciplined, but when they were older, they might be whipped by a specially appointed community whipper. Children often were named after notable ancestors, with the hope that the child would develop similar qualities, and name-giving ceremonies, with the giving of gifts, marked the event. Nicknames also were given, and later in a person's life, new names might be acquired to recognize an important deed, a personal attribute, or the guardian spirit. Names were considered private possessions of the person or the family.

Between the ages of three and six, girls learned to use toy digging sticks and boys were instructed in the use of small bows and arrows. Special ceremonies celebrated a boy's first game kill and a girl's first root-digging and berry-picking. About the same time, they received a serious formal lecture from a prominent elder about correct conduct and morals. As they approached adolescence, they were instructed by their parents and a shaman about religious beliefs and practices.

Like most other Native Americans, the Nez Perce were animists; they believed that everything in creation—animals, birds, fish, rocks, trees, stars, planets, and all natural phenomena—had spirits, or a supernatural side, that appeared to humans in visions and could influence them for good or harm. Through vision quests humans acquired personal guardian spirits, sometimes called tutelary, or teaching, spirits, who conferred on them certain powers, or spiritually supported abilities, that had a separate existence from the individual. The vision of a deer, for instance, would endow one with swiftness; hunting powers would improve the chances of a hunter; and powers needed in war would help a warrior.

In a vision, the spirit might appear as a human, but with the attributes of its animal or other natural form. The spirit would explain the nature of its powers and instruct the vision-seeker in things that he or she must and must not do to receive the spirit's support through life. The individual also received a personal spirit song to be used with proper rituals to summon the spirit. If a person abused his power or broke a taboo before seeking the spirit, the power could cause bad luck, an accident, illness, or death.

Sometimes after reaching the age of nine, youths were left alone at a remote place, often on a mountaintop, to seek a vision and acquire a guardian spirit, a *wé·yekın*. They went without food, perhaps for days, until they either had a vision that revealed the spirit or until they could no longer maintain the vigil. Failure to receive a vision usually meant a mediocre or difficult life, and some youths went on vision quests more than once. A person who received a very strong power recognized by the shamans would be trained by them to become a shaman. Pretense at having had a vision was avoided for fear of punishment by the offended spirit.

The youths would reveal the identity of their guardian spirits by singing their spirit songs for the first time at a special dance ceremony, presided over by the shamans and lasting from five to ten days in the winter. Thereafter, they would use a name and wear and carry objects symbolic of their *wé·yekın*, whose aid they would seek throughout their lives. The shamans, known as *tıwé·t*, were wise and respected people. Besides being in charge of most rituals, which in effect kept the people loyal to the ongoing society, they served as doctors, or curers, foretellers of the future, locators of game, controllers of the weather, and advisers. They acquired their authority from their ability to communicate with the spiritual world and often had many guardian spirits, but much of their power and success came from their knowledge of the curing power of plants, their understanding of human nature and of how to deal with people, and their skill at sorcery. They included both men and women and often had an association of their own within a large band.

When they reached puberty, Nez Perce girls were isolated for a week in special menstrual lodges, and at a marriageable age they were courted if they had not previously been betrothed. Marriages usually took place between members of families of equal prestige and per-

sonal wealth. Relatives—even distant cousins—were not permitted
to marry each other. When a young man indicated that he wished
to marry a certain girl, the girl's behavior was observed to see if she
would make a good wife. If all was well, a go-between would arrange
the marriage and the couple would live together for a while to be
sure they were compatible. Then a date was set for ceremonial exchanges of gifts between the two families. The groom's relatives were
hosts of the first exchange. Six months later, it was the turn of the
bride's family. On completion of the two gift exchanges, the couple
was recognized as married. A husband might also take his wife's sister
as a second wife; in any case, he usually was expected to marry her
if his wife died. Conversely, a widow usually married her deceased
husband's oldest brother. Divorce was easy to obtain, and the individuals returned to their respective kin groups.

Besides spirits, humans, as well as natural objects, were believed
to have souls, without which they died. If a Nez Perce properly observed rituals during life, his soul would successfully reach an afterworld where life continued. The Nez Perce did not believe in a better
"happy hunting ground" or a hell. When a soul departed and a person died, female relatives set up a wailing, or keening. The corpse was
ritually bathed and buried with some of the dead person's possessions
that might be needed in the afterworld. Shamans performed rituals
to keep the ghost of the deceased from returning to haunt the village,
and relatives distributed the departed one's remaining property. The
surviving spouse went into mourning for a year and was then able to
remarry. Anything that recalled the deceased, even a house or sweat
lodge, was sometimes destroyed, and the person's name was not again
mentioned unless it was bestowed on a new, young member of the
family.

Throughout their lives, the Nez Perce lived close to nature and
respected it. The earth was their mother from which they came and
to which they returned. Her life and products enabled them to live,
and they gave thanks to the spirits of whatever they took so that they
would reappear.

Because of their numbers and organization, their wide-ranging habits, their large and varied food supply, which gave them many things to trade, and their geographical position between the peoples of the Plateau region and those of the northern plains, the Nez Perce by 1700 were perhaps the most influential people of the Plateau. But that influence was to become even greater with the arrival of the white man in the Northwest.

Chapter Two
Omens of Change

Long before they saw the first white men, the Nez Perce began to feel their influences. Russians first appeared on the Alaskan coast only in the 1740s, and European and American seamen did not begin to trade with tribes along the Pacific Coast south of Alaska until several decades later. But Spaniards, who had been in the Southwest since 1540, had established a permanent colony in New Mexico in 1590 and had probed many times into the southern plains, the Great Basin, and California, meeting many tribes. Starting in the seventeenth century, moreover, British and French fur traders had been moving westward from Hudson Bay and the Great Lakes, and Frenchmen had explored the eastern fringes of the plains. All of them had had contact with tribes in the heartland of the continent to whom they had introduced guns, knives, axes, cloth, and other manufactured goods. Descriptions of these newcomers and their possessions and powers had undoubtedly been passed across the plains and mountains from tribe to tribe until, at some unknown time, diffused knowledge of the whites reached the Nez Perce villagers and other Plateau peoples.

Whether odd pieces of Spanish goods had traveled northward from New Mexico to the Plateau region prior to 1700 via a trade contact chain of tribes is not known. But about 1730, or slightly earlier, horses had reached the Nez Perce from that direction. After the Ice Age, horses had become extinct in the Western Hemisphere, but Columbus had reintroduced them in the Americas. In 1680, during a Pueblo revolt against the Spaniards in New Mexico, a large number of horses fell into Indian hands. Thereafter, by trade or through raids,

the animals spread northward from tribe to tribe on both sides of the
Rocky Mountains.

Traditional lore among the Nez Perce says that they first saw
horses among their close relatives and allies, the Cayuses of Oregon.
Learning that they had been acquired from the Shoshonis, they sent a
group south to trade for some. It is estimated that it took a generation
for a people to become fully adjusted to the use of the horse, but in
time all Nez Perce became mounted and found the horse a valuable
addition to their lives.

The abundance of nutritious grasses in Nez Perce Country favored the increase of the animals. In the summer, the high, green
meadows offered huge areas of pasture, and when it turned cold, the
people could drive the horses down toward their villages in the protected valleys and canyons that provided protein-rich bunchgrass,
willows, and other forage for winter. Wild animals that normally attacked horses were relatively few in the region, and the many rim-
rocked chasms and densely wooded mountains kept the horses from
dispersing and moving elsewhere. The herds became so large—with
certain bands possessing more than a thousand horses and prominent
individuals several hundred—that most whites reaching the interior
of the Northwest in the early nineteenth century commented with
awe on the immense number.

Wherever conditions were favorable in the Plateau region, horses
multiplied, and other tribes built up big herds. At the same time,
on the eastern side of the Rockies, horses went from the Mountain,
or Eastern, Shoshonis to the Flatheads and Kutenais and eventually,
from those three and the Nez Perce to the Blackfeet tribes on the
northern plains. By the mid-1700s, nearly all the tribes usually met
by the Nez Perce were mounted. Large, milling herds were a familiar
sight at intertribal gatherings.

Almost alone among all the native peoples on the continent the
Nez Perce practiced selective breeding. No one knows how they acquired the skill, although it has been surmised that one or more of the
far-ranging members of the tribe may have spent some time among
the Spaniards in the Southwest. In their own region, they were the

only Indians who became horse breeders, and they did so remarkably quickly. In 1806, during the visit of Lewis and Clark, a Nez Perce gelded some of the expedition's horses, and, following the swift recovery of the animals, Lewis noted surprisedly, "I have no hesitation in declaring my belief that the indian method of gelding is preferable to that practiced by ourselves." Yet the Nez Perce had owned horses for less than 100 years. The story that they specially bred spotted horses, known today as Appaloosas, as war horses is a widespread myth that arose in the 1930s as part of a campaign to make them commercially popular. The Nez Perce favored and bred any color or kind of horse so long as it was swift and intelligent and pleased them.

The horse brought many changes to the Nez Perce. The people could now travel farther and for longer periods of time, transporting more supplies, trade goods, and provisions, as well as longer tipi poles for larger and roomier portable lodges. They were able to reach and intensify their use of more distant and less accessible fishing, gathering, and hunting sites, and their hunts in the rugged plateau country became easier and more extended and successful. Their increased ability at collecting food supplies gave them more leisure time, which allowed more time for travel. As they extended their horizons and increased their trade, they acquired more goods from other peoples, as well as many new ideas and elements of material culture that influenced and altered their lives.

Their heightened contacts with the more westerly tribes brought them bigger supplies of fish oil, dried shellfish, baskets, carved wooden implements, wapatoo roots, and a variety of shells, and from a Great Basin people, they now apparently adopted the use of a new and effective small, side-notched arrowhead. The greatest impacts on them, however, came from dramatically increased and broadened relations with the plains tribes in the east. With horses, many more Nez Perce than before left their villages in the late spring or early summer to travel across the Bitterroot Mountains to hunt buffalo. The parties, often band-sized and under strong leaders, stayed on the plains for six months to two years, frequently with Flatheads and Kutenais. As they roamed across the northern and central plains prior to their first known contacts with whites, they met and traded with friendly bands of Eastern Shoshonis and many other tribes and, on occasion, clashed with some, particularly the Blackfeet, Cheyennes, and Crows.

The Nez Perce had long hunted bison, both west and east of the mountains, and had used parts of the animal for robes, utensils, and other products. But buffalo hunting on foot had been a relatively minor part of the cultural life of most of the people and had made little impact on the economy or Plateau Culture of the river-oriented villagers. With the arrival of the horse and the growing number of people who rode to the buffalo country, however, traits and customs of the plains way of life were increasingly developed or adopted. Nez Perce packed their horses with berries and roots, cakes of camas, dried fish, salmon oil in sealed fish skins, bows of mountain sheep horn, seashells, mountain grass hemp, and other products of the Northwest and traded them on the plains for dressed buffalo robes, rawhide skins, buffalo-hide lodge covers, beads, feathered bonnets, stone pipes, and various goods that had come from farther east in intertribal trade. With horses, they could transport these articles home, and gradually the traditional Plateau-based economy became overlain with elements that gave it a plains coloration.

These were the formative days of what eventually developed into the full-blown, classic Plains Culture of the nineteenth century. Many tribes had only recently migrated onto the plains from the eastern woodlands or western mountains and deserts, and most of them, like the Nez Perce, had just acquired the horse. None of the northern or central plains tribes yet had guns, though some would shortly begin to receive them from British and French fur traders and eastern tribes. The Nez Perce participated in the development of the historic Plains Culture, contributing to it as well as receiving many ideas and influences. They increased their use of buffalo meat, substituted buffalo hides for grass mats as covers for portable conical tipis, employed numerous buffalo-bone implements and tools, fashioned painted plains-style rawhide bags and pouches, and adopted feathered headdresses, vests, plains dances and songs, and new details of dress ornamentation, including the use of hair as shirt decoration.

They enriched the Plains Culture with their own products, including horn bows, otter-skin sashes, one-skin poncho shirts, long two-skin shirts and dresses, and fur caps of mountain goat, wolf, and ermine, ornamented with horns, bird feathers, and shells.

At the same time, the Nez Perce adopted many elements of the plains war complex. On the plains, bands raided each other for horses, trophies, honors, and captives, and the raids produced counter-raids for retaliation and the freeing of prisoners and retaking of stolen property. Young Nez Perce males grouped themselves around the ablest and most valiant warriors, who became figures of prestige and power, and tried to advance their own position by such exploits as counting coup, stealing horses, or killing an enemy. Strong war chiefs emerged, who if they were not also the leaders of the bands, were given full authority in hunts and during war emergencies. They were usually elevated to their status by a band's association of warriors, whose members also engaged in special rituals, conducted initiations, and were generally responsible for war activities. The warrior society members pledged themselves never to retreat, and in battle many of them planted staffs in the ground and fought until they were relieved or the fighting had ended. Through the years, many Nez Perce distinguished themselves by bravery, and tribal lore still celebrates stirring war exploits on the plains, as well as against the Nez Perce enemies in the south, by such heroic chiefs and warriors of the past as Ká·ʔawapu· (Man of the Dawn), ʔɩpelí·kt hɩlú·mkewe·t (The Cloud Gatherer), Wé·yux tí·menɩ́n (Marked Legs), Pá·qata·s ʔewyí·n (Five Wounds), X̣áx̣a·c ʔɩlṗílp (Red Grizzly Bear), Tuna-kehm-mu-toolt (Broken Arm), Mɩtá·t wé·tes (Three Lands), and Noose-nu Pahk-kah-tim (Cut Nose).

In the camps on the plains, as well as in the villages back home after a band's return, the people honored courageous warriors, mourned those who were slain, and held war and feather dances, ceremonials, and parades. Horses were painted and decorated with elaborate trappings of rawhide, horse hair, and bone and antler, ornamented with porcupine quills and beads. Warriors and hunters rode bareback or on small saddle blankets, but the tribe, as a whole, possessed and often used different saddles for men and women and for packing animals. The saddles and horse gear frequently showed a Spanish influence, which had been transmitted from the Southwest with the horses.

Not all Nez Perce villagers went to the plains, and the degree of plains influence differed in various regions. Where horses were in most use and the people traveled most often to the plains, economic class distinctions appeared. Horses were considered personal property and objects of wealth. They could be exchanged as gifts and bought and sold by barter, as well as acquired in raids, and men of distinction were often able to increase their status and power by owning a large number of horses. On the whole, also, the size of herds tended to augment economic differences between bands, so some were deemed less powerful than others. Horses in some cases affected population distribution and settlement patterns. Some villages and bands frequented, or shifted to, better grazing grounds or sites where they could more effectively care for or utilize the animals. With people away on long travels some villages and band areas were abandoned, or partly so, for up to two years. Among some bands that rode regularly to the plains, the ties between the people grew stronger through marriage and other associations, and the villages combined. Some of them were given up, and others became larger. Those bands most affected were along the Clearwater River and its tributaries, while those least affected were farther south in the deep canyon countries of the Snake and Salmon rivers, where the old Plateau Culture continued strongly.

In the middle of the eighteenth century, conflict on the northern plains intensified between the Nez Perce, Flatheads, Kutenais, and Eastern Shoshonis on the one side and the confederated Blackfeet tribes on the other. The Nez Perce and the other western tribes had supplied the Blackfeet with most of their horses, either through peaceful trade or as the result of raids, but about 1755, the Blackfeet tribes, comprising the Piegans, Bloods, and Blackfoot proper, together with their allies, the Atsinas and Sarcis, began to receive British and French guns through fur trade channels in Canada. Without white men's arms, the Nez Perce and their allies were thrown on the defensive and over a period of years lost many people and horses and were almost driven back into the Rocky Mountains.

A large disaster struck the Nez Perce and other tribes in 1781–82. White traders inadvertently introduced smallpox to some eastern tribes, and the sickness spread across the plains with devastating effects to many tribes, including the Blackfeet, the Nez Perce and Flatheads, and other peoples on the Great Plains and the Plateau, none of whom had defenses against diseases which the white men had brought from Europe. The Blackfeet apparently lost about half of their people, and Nez Perce losses may have been as great, or nearly so. At times within the next twenty years, it is conjectured, epidemics coming possibly from white sea traders on the Pacific Coast or from Spaniards in the Southwest also ravaged the Nez Perce and other northwestern tribes.

The 1781–82 epidemic undoubtedly decimated Nez Perce villages, stripped the people of some of their headmen and prominent leaders, undermined and weakened their societies, and for a time demoralized the survivors. Some anthropologists maintain that in reaction a temporary "prophet cult," centering around one or more religious leaders who announced prophecies received in visions, swept through the Plateau. Such a cult, it is asserted, was not only a response to the traumatic shock of their population losses, but reflected also a conflicting combination of their anxiety over the approaching white men, who had introduced the disease and had many other great powers, as well as of their desire to meet the whites because they would be bringing with them many wondrous gifts. Evidence of such a transient cult among the Nez Perce at this time is scanty and subject to controversy, however, even though archeological findings of abrupt changes in Nez Perce burial patterns and habits in the eighteenth century and a possible preoccupation with death among Plateau peoples have been advanced to support its existence.

There is no doubt, at any rate, that by the late eighteenth century the Nez Perce were aware that the whites were the source of many strange and desirable possessions, including guns, powder and balls, knives, ironware, and other articles. Some of the white men's goods, in fact, had already made their way, by trade or stealth in warfare, into the Nez Perce Country from the east, the south, or the Pacific Coast. They included Spanish coins and bridles, blue and white beads, blankets, cloth, and pieces of brass and copper, some of which the Nez Perce cut up and made into cone jingles and ornamentals. The Eastern Shoshonis and Nez Perce, in addition, are known already to have had a name for the white men whom they had yet to see. The Shoshonis referred to them as *so·yá·po·*, and the Nez Perce called them *ʔalláyma*. Both terms meant "people of the long knives or big blades" and were probably derived from similar expressions that more easterly tribes used.

Immediately prior to 1800 some Nez Perce, taken prisoner by other tribes on the Montana plains and brought to trade centers on the Saskatchewan or Missouri rivers, were the first of their people known to have set eyes on whites. Among them, according to a Nez Perce story, was a woman who became known as Wetxu·wí·s, which meant "returned home from a far-away place." She had been sold from tribe to tribe and eventually to a French Canadian or mixed blood, with whom she lived for a while among whites in central Canada. She was treated kindly and given medicine to help her trachoma, a contagious eye disease that was prevalent among the Nez Perce, but in time things did not go well for her. She ran away and after many adventures, managed to return safely to her own people on the Clearwater River. When the Lewis and Clark expedition arrived in Nez Perce Country in 1805, Clark saw her, but he was not told that she had advised her fellow-villagers to receive the white visitors with friendship. "These are the people who helped me" tribal tradition quotes her as counseling the Nez Perce. "Do them no hurt."

It is possible that awareness of the steady movement of the whites toward them, coupled with the shock of population losses from epidemics, filled the Nez Perce with anxiety and apprehension. But it is clear that their desire for white men's goods, especially guns and ammunition with which to counter their enemies, increased. In the first years of the nineteenth century, they may have been aware from the Kutenais and Flatheads of attempts by English fur traders to get past the Blackfeet and cross the Rocky Mountains into the Plateau country. It seems probable that they looked for guns from those traders, for Nez Perce parties from time to time traveled north with the Kutenais and Flatheads, searching for whites. Finally, in the spring of 1805, even as the Lewis and Clark expedition was heading west on the Missouri River, a group of Nez Perce managed to reach the home villages of the Hidatsa, or Gros Ventre, Indians near present-day Bismarck, North Dakota, and buy six guns from them. The Nez Perce got safely back to their band in the Kamiah Valley in Idaho with the guns, and when Lewis and Clark were at Kamiah, they gave the Indians powder and balls for the weapons.

Lewis and Clark entered the Nez Perce Country in September 1805. Having ascended the Missouri River to its head, they were seeking navigable waters to the Pacific. The rugged canyon of Idaho's Salmon River had rebuffed them and, traveling north to Montana's Bitterroot Valley, they had struck westward across the wilds of the Bitterroot Mountains on horses bartered from the Eastern Shoshonis. Though two Shoshonis helped them follow the high Lolo Trail, which the Nez Perce customarily used in going to the buffalo country, the season was late, and the expedition members floundered in snowstorms and almost starved. After extreme privations, an advance party of Clark and six hunters descended on September 20 to the snow-free meadows of Weippe Prairie where a fall encampment of Nez Perce was gathering camas roots.

"At the distance of 1 mile from the lodges," wrote Clark of this first encounter, "I met 3 Indian boys, when they saw me [they] ran and hid themselves, in the grass I desmounted gave my gun and horse to one of the men, searched in the grass and found 2 of the boys gave them Small pieces of ribin & sent them forward to the village Soon after a man Came out to meet me with great caution & Conducted me to a large Spacious Lodge . . . those people gave us a Small piece of Buffalow meat, Some dried beries & roots in different States . . . I gave them a fiew Small articles as preasants."

The encampment was apparently that of Kamiah area villagers, and Clark learned that the band's great head chief, Tuna-kehm-mu-toolt, or Broken Arm, together with all the warriors, had left three days before in a southwesterly direction to fight their enemies, the Tɪwélqe. These were the Western Shoshonis, Paiutes, and Bannocks, all of whom, together with the Eastern Shoshonis, Lewis and Clark and other whites had learned from more easterly tribes to refer to as Snake Indians. The great chief and the warriors were not expected back for another fifteen or eighteen days.

Guided by the Nez Perce, who provided food, Clark the next day reached the Clearwater River at present-day Greer and 3 kilometers (2 miles) downstream stopped at a village whose elderly headman was ʔá·lya?, which Clark understood meant The Twisted Hair. It was in this village that Wetxu·wí·s, the woman who had returned from the east, saw the whites and told her people to do the strangers no harm. Possibly for this reason, the Nez Perce showed the small band of explorers friendship and hospitality. The Twisted Hair welcomed them and the next day accompanied them back to Weippe Prairie where Lewis and the rest of the expedition had arrived weak and starving.

Though many of the whites became temporarily ill from dysentery, the food generously supplied them by the Nez Perce saved their lives, and they gradually regained their strength. At the same time, The Twisted Hair and other Nez Perce made maps on whitened elk skins to show them the water route ahead. Escorted by some Nez Perce—whom Lewis and Clark called the Chopunnish, which may have been a corruption of Sahaptian—they made their way down the Clearwater to a point opposite the mouth of the North Fork of that river, where they halted long enough to construct dugout canoes. On October 7, after caching some of their supplies and entrusting their horses to members of The Twisted Hair's family until they returned the next year, they left what is now known as Canoe Camp and set off down the Clearwater in the canoes.

They passed many small Nez Perce winter villages and fishing camps and at the site of present-day Lewiston turned into the Snake River. The two Eastern Shoshonis who had conducted them over the Bitterroot Mountains had meanwhile returned to their own tribe, but

The Twisted Hair and another Nez Perce man went along with them down the Snake and Columbia rivers, helping them negotiate with the new peoples through whose countries they passed. At the great Dalles fishing center, the explorers finally parted with the two helpful Nez Perce and continued their journey to the Pacific Ocean.

The following spring, the explorers started up the Columbia again on their return trip home and by May 1806 were back among the Nez Perce on the Clearwater River. They recovered most of their horses from The Twisted Hair, who told them that the great war chiefs, who had missed them the previous fall, wanted to meet them.

The explorers distributed trade medals and American flags to the chiefs, and with the help of their Eastern Shoshoni traveling companion, Sacajawea, and a Western Shoshoni, who had been captured by the Nez Perce and spoke the Nez Perce language, described the powerful American nation in the east which they represented and the expedition's purposes. One goal, they explained, was to establish peace among all warring tribes so that they could erect trading houses where the people could go in safety and secure white men's goods.

The chiefs were skeptical that their enemies would agree to peace, but the prospect of being able to acquire white men's arms and other goods was appealing, and they said that they would consider the proposal.

The chiefs finally agreed to recommend to their bands "confidence in the information they had received" from Lewis and Clark. Broken Arm addressed all the people, "making known the deliberations of their council and impressing the necessity of unanimity among them." There was not a dissenting vote, and an old civil chief, who Lewis understood was the father of Red Grizzly Bear, told the explorers that the Nez Perce were "convinced of the advantages of peace and ardently wished to cultivate peace with their neighbors." He concluded with the promise "that the whitemen might be assured of their warmest attachment and that they would always give them every assistance in their power; that they were poor but their hearts were good."

Within the context of the history of future relations between the

Nez Perce and white men, this council and the Nez Perce promise of friendship and alliance with the Americans had an enduring significance. Word of the agreement was spread among the villages, and knowledge was passed from generation to generation that the Nez Perce leaders had given their word to Lewis and Clark, the first white men in their country. The Nez Perce who could later say that they had met or seen the American captains boasted about it with increasing pride and saw to it that the younger people understood the promise given in the Kamiah Valley, and that they honored it. Despite persecution and pressure, the tribe's friendship for Americans would persist with few interruptions until 1877, and white men in their country lived in debt to the spirit of friendship and mutual trust that existed between the Lewis and Clark Expedition and its Nez Perce hosts.

Chapter Three
The Fur Traders

Because of snow in the mountains, the Lewis and Clark expedition camped for several weeks among the Nez Perce in the Kamiah Valley. The longer the explorers were with the Nez Perce, the higher grew their regard for them. The Nez Perce "has shown much greater acts of hospitality than we have witnessed from any nation or tribe since we have passed the rocky mountains," Clark wrote. Early in June, the expedition members, guided by five Nez Perce, finally left their Long Camp site near Kamiah and successfully re-crossed the Bitterroots to Montana.

On his way home, Meriwether Lewis tried to contact the Blackfeet to talk them into halting their warfare against the Nez Perce and western tribes, but he failed. A brief meeting with some Piegans, in fact, almost cost Lewis his life and only served to warn those Indians that Americans intended to open trade for goods, including arms, with their enemies west of the mountains.

As though it were a direct result of the promise of Lewis and Clark, however, fur traders from both Canada and the United States soon afterward began to get past the Blackfoot barrier and appear among the Nez Perce and other Plateau tribes. Beginning in 1807, David Thompson and other traders and employees of the Canadian North West Company, having finally found a pass across the Canadian Rockies, turned south and coursed their way along many of the rivers of the Northwest, building fur posts and opening trade for furs, provisions, horses, and supplies with the Kutenais, Flatheads, Spokans, and others. The Canadians did not at first find their way into

Nez Perce Country, but the Nez Perce quickly learned of their presence and traveled to trade at posts the whites had built. On March 11, 1810, Thompson noted in his journal at the Saleesh House, a post he had erected in the Flatheads' country on the Clark Fork River near present-day Thompson Falls, Montana, "Traded a very trifle of provisions from the Nez Perce." It is the earliest-known use of that name for the tribe and appears to be the term being used by Thompson's French-speaking trappers, who believed they saw some of the Nez Perce wearing bits of shell in their noses. By that same spring, Thompson's records also show that he had already traded more than twenty guns to the western Indians, and that summer a war party of 150 Nez Perce and Flatheads used their new weapons to drive off an enemy group of Piegans on the Montana plains.

In the meantime, American trappers and traders, many of them inspired by Lewis and Clark's reports of abundant beaver in the Rocky Mountains and the Northwest, were also heading west, traveling up the Missouri or across the northern plains. For a time, the Blackfeet and their allies had more success in interfering with their trade with the western tribes, killing many of the Americans, driving them back or dispersing their parties. There is evidence of one large but little known group of forty-two Americans being wiped out to a man by Blackfeet in northwestern Montana about 1807 after having traded with the Nez Perce. Others seem to have met and traded with buffalo-hunting groups of Nez Perce on the plains from Montana to southeastern Idaho. In general, the white Americans came to regard the Nez Perce and Flatheads as friends and the Blackfeet as mortal enemies.

In 1811 a teen-aged Massachusetts trapper named Archibald Pelton seems to have wandered through southern Idaho in a crazed condition after Blackfoot attacks on his party. Eventually, Nez Perce found him, and he spent part of the year living in a Nez Perce village on the Clearwater River. Late that winter he was discovered by the first party of white traders known to have entered the Nez Perce Country—a ragged and starving group of eleven members of John Jacob Astor's Pacific Fur Company. They were part of a larger body that had come overland from St. Louis under Wilson Price Hunt to erect a fur post at the mouth of the Columbia River. After many accidents and misfortunes in southern Idaho, they had disintegrated into smaller groups, and 11 men under a Herculean, 136-kilo (300-pound) trader named Donald McKenzie had struggled north through part of Hells Canyon of the Snake River and across the mountains to the Nez Perce villages.

The Nez Perce were as friendly and hospitable to them as they had been to Lewis and Clark, and when McKenzie and his men regained their strength and set off down the Columbia, they promised to return and open a trading post among the Nez Perce. McKenzie was as good as his word. In August 1812 he erected a small Pacific Fur Company post on the north side of the Clearwater River 8 kilometers (5 miles) above present-day Lewiston. The project was not successful. The Nez Perce were willing to trade things they owned or produced, like clothing, food, and horses, but they were not willing to become beaver trappers and laborers for the whites. At the same time, McKenzie's men were high-handed and demanding. Soon tension and an icy hostility developed between them. Increasing numbers of competitors were arriving in the Plateau country from Canada, and when news circulated that the United States and Great Britain had begun the hostilities of the War of 1812, McKenzie closed the Clearwater post and withdrew to the Pacific Fur Company's main post, Astoria, at the mouth of the Columbia. On October 16, 1813, the Astorians, threatened by the superior number of their competitors and by word that an English warship was on its way to the Columbia, sold out to the North West Company and the next year left the Northwest.

Meanwhile, during the evacuation, a hot-tempered Astorian trader, John Clarke, had had an altercation with a group of Nez Perce and Palouse Indians at the mouth of the Palouse River on the Snake in southwestern Washington and had hanged one of them. The brutal action had outraged the Nez Perce and other tribes and had turned them against all whites, and for a while violent confrontations occurred between the Sahaptian-speaking peoples and the North West

Company employees who were trying to develop the trade opportunities purchased from the Astorians. Peace was finally reestablished in 1814. But the whites stayed away from Nez Perce Country, and the Nez Perce had to barter for guns, ammunition, and other goods with the Spokans, Flatheads, and others among whom the North West Company maintained trading posts. Despite this indirect method, white men's goods streamed into many Nez Perce villages, enriching their material culture.

In 1816 Donald McKenzie, now in the employ of the North West Company, returned to the Northwest and, after making peace with the Nez Perce, built a substantial fur post on the Columbia near the mouth of the Walla Walla River, about 19 kilometers (12 miles) below the confluence of the Snake and Columbia, which he called Fort Nez Perce. Here he intended to trade with the Nez Perce, as well as the Cayuses, Wallawallas, Palouses, and other tribes in the vicinity. At the same time, he initiated a new era of leading brigades from the fort through various regions of the Northwest to do their own trapping. The brigades, composed of French-Canadian, Hawaiian, English, American, and eastern Iroquois Indian employees of the North West Company, concentrated initially on the Snake River country of southern Idaho and for a time were caught in the continuing warfare between the Nez Perce and Cayuses and their Western Shoshoni and Bannock enemies. By patient negotiations, however, McKenzie was at last able to bring about an enduring peace between them, and from time to time bands of each of those tribes began to camp with and help provision the brigades. The enterprising McKenzie also tried to find a faster route between Fort Nez Perce and the beaver country of southern Idaho. In 1818, with six Canadians, he tested using the Snake River and for two months pushed, pulled, and portaged his boats through the entire length of Hells Canyon. He was so shaken by the experience that he never tried it again, nor did anyone else ever repeat the feat.

Though few Nez Perce ever took to trapping beaver themselves, they found a market for their horses, food supplies, and various products at Fort Nez Perce, and some increasingly frequented that post.

In 1821 the British Hudson's Bay Company merged with the North West Company and the next year changed its policy to having its fur-gathering brigades depart from its post in the Flatheads' country of northwestern Montana and work their way down to southern Idaho through the beaver-rich valleys on the eastern side of the Bitterroot Mountains. The change brought them into close contact with the buffalo-hunting bands of Nez Perce, who regularly roamed through much of that country with the Flatheads and Kutenais and who now periodically attached themselves to the bridges, greatly increasing their trade for firearms and other manufactured goods, and joining whites in skirmishes with their mutual enemies, the Blackfeet and Atsinas.

Beginning in 1824, Jedediah Smith, William Sublette, and other American trappers and traders from St. Louis entered the area and by outbidding the Hudson's Bay Company greatly enhanced the Indians' position. At Fort Nez Perce and in their own country, the Nez Perce continued to sell the British horses and provisions, but on the plains the bands increasingly transferred their friendship and allegiance to the "bigger-hearted" Americans. The appearance of the Americans created the beginning of a crisis for the Hudson's Bay Company. Since 1818 Great Britain and the United States had observed a joint occu-pancy of the Oregon Country, with freedom within it for citizens of both nations. Although the British had operated without competi-tion from the Americans since the departure of the Astorians, it was evident that a growing number of Americans would now be appear-ing. Believing that the joint occupancy would end in 1828, and that the two nations would then divide the territory, with the Columbia River as the boundary, the Hudson's Bay Company made plans to move all its posts, including Fort Nez Perce, to the northern side of the Columbia and by 1828 trap to exhaustion all of southern Idaho, which would become American-owned.

Joint occupancy actually did not end until 1846, and then the boundary line was the 49th parallel, far north of the Columbia. Meanwhile, opposition by the Nez Perce and other tribes forced the British to abandon plans to move Fort Nez Perce. But at the same time, in 1826, they built a large new post, Fort Colvile, in what they thought would be secure British territory in the northeastern part of the present state of Washington. Their efforts to trap out the so-called snake country of southern Idaho and outbid the Americans failed to halt the influx of American trappers or the wavering loyalty of the tribes. The bands continued to move back and forth between the white competitors, looking for the highest prices for their products, but generally the Nez Perce and their Flathead allies preferred traveling and trading with the democratic, easygoing American mountain men, who often paid no attention to fixed prices, as the British company traders were forced to do, but offered goods as free agents in accordance with their needs and desires. Nez Perce buffalo-hunting bands wintered in sheltered valleys with the Americans, fought side by side with them against the Blackfeet, and frequently permitted Nez Perce women to become the wives of trappers. Starting in 1827, the Nez Perce, together with Flatheads and Eastern Shoshonis, showed up regularly at the Americans' rendezvous, sharing in the celebrations, feasting, gambling, and general jollity of those annual summer gatherings of the fur men. At the 1832 rendezvous, held in Pierre's Hole (the present-day Teton Basin) in southeastern Idaho, seven Nez Perce and Flatheads were killed and many others wounded fighting alongside white trappers and traders in a ferocious all-day battle against an interloping war party of Atsina Indians.

In their homeland the Nez Perce villagers, still with only supplies and horses to trade, continued to attract the attention of few whites. Occasionally, a small party of American trappers would appear out of the mountains, visit briefly, and go on. Some Hudson's Bay Company traders based at the old Fort Nez Perce, which the British were beginning to call Fort Walla Walla, would travel occasionally to Nez Perce villages to buy horses. In 1831 a Nez Perce guided a brigade under John Work across the Lolo Trail to Montana.

The Nez Perce, however, were at a turning point in their history. They were armed adequately with guns and could acquire whatever goods they wanted from whites. Their strength, and the sources of their supplies, gave them confidence that they could hold their own on contested buffalo grounds, even in the territory of their enemies. The trade goods they acquired on the plains and at the posts were steadily enriching their material lives, and no one threatened their villages or their customs. Their wealth and their geographic position close to the plains helped increase their status as the strongest and most influential people of the Plateau.

But in this heyday the seed of a disruptive change was being planted. The closeness with white Americans was affecting some Nez Perce. A dependence on the whites was growing, and a few Nez Perce curried favors and gifts from them and almost seemed as if they wanted to live and be like the whites themselves. On March 1, 1833, a Methodist publication in New York City carried a dramatic article about four Indians who had journeyed from the Rocky Mountains to St. Louis in 1831, allegedly seeking information about the white man's religion. Those Indians were Nez Perce. Although the article was based largely on misunderstanding, it was to have profound effects on all the Nez Perce people.

Chapter Four
Agents of Change

Some anthropologists, notably Deward E. Walker Jr., believe that certain Christian ideas may have diffused into the Plateau region as early as the eighteenth century, prior to the whites' arrival, and influenced some of the beliefs and practices of a "prophet cult" among the Nez Perce. The cult, according to Walker, included a number of Christian-like features: beliefs in a single creator God and sub-deities resembling angels; a hereafter, "entrance to which was determined largely by the morality of actions in this world;" and a book, the Bible, that contained valuable information. Its practices, moreover, are thought to have included worship services conducted around a flagpole by a religious leader; the use of special songs and dances in the services; the observance of the Sabbath; and emphasis on a moral code of charitable behavior. Though the cult may have waned before the arrival of Lewis and Clark, who made no mention of it, Walker suggests that it never died out but, with modifications, continued to underlie and account for much of the Nez Perce later history.

Many Nez Perce have maintained that before the coming of whites, their ancestors did believe in a supernatural being above all other spirits, a single God, who was the Creator and Maker of the universe. Whether this stemmed from the existence of a pre-contact cult with Christian influences is not known. When Lewis and Clark and the trappers and traders finally did reach the Northwest, the Nez Perce began to hear at first hand of the whites' religious beliefs, seeing some of the more devout explorers and fur men at prayer and watching them read from their Bibles. In the countries of the Spokans and Flatheads and while traveling with the fur brigades, Nez Perce met Catholic French-Canadian and Iroquois Indian trappers who told them about their beliefs. And at fur posts like Fort Nez Perce, they became familiar with the observance of the Sabbath and Christmas, when a flag flew from the flagpole and the fur men shaved, dressed differently, celebrated, and did no work. The whites' religion undoubtedly aroused curiosity and interest among some Nez Perce, particularly the prestige-seeking headmen and chiefs, who understood from their own system of vision quests and guardian spirits that achievement of secular goals came from supernatural power. Nevertheless, for more than two decades in the nineteenth century, Christianity seems to have made little or no impact on the Nez Perce.

Then a dramatic train of events occurred. In 1825 the Hudson's Bay Company sent sons of important Spokan and Kutenai headmen to an Anglican mission school at Red River, at present-day Winnipeg, Canada. After four years of Christian training, they returned to their homes, speaking English, dressed like whites, and carrying Bibles. They became sensations in their villages, and throughout the winter of 1829–30 both of them, particularly Spokan Garry (named for Nicholas Garry, a Hudson's Bay Company official), lectured and preached forcefully to large groups of Indians from many Plateau tribes, including the Nez Perce.

The youths' readings from the Bible and explanations about the Ten Commandments, the need to observe Sunday, and other basic Christian teachings made a great impression on their Nez Perce listeners. Viewing this knowledge of a relationship to the supernatural world, different from their own, as a source of the white men's economic and social power, and envious perhaps of its acquisition by the Spokans and Kutenais, some Nez Perce headmen quickly became desirous of possessing the information, especially a copy of the Bible, the book that seemed to contain all the instructions they would need to know.

As a result, when the Hudson's Bay Company announced that its fur men would escort more young Indians to the Red River mission for training in 1830, the Nez Perce eagerly sent two youths. One, whom the whites named Ellice for another Hudson's Bay Company official, was the grandson of the prominent old war chief, Red Grizzly Bear. The next year, 1831, in an even more significant development, four venturesome Nez Perce warriors from a buffalo-hunting band, whose home villages were on the upper Clearwater, joined a group of American fur traders under Lucien Fontenelle who were returning from Utah to Missouri. In St. Louis, they met William Clark, who had become Superintendent of Indian Affairs, and the Catholic Bishop, Joseph Rosati, and they created the impression that they had been sent by their people to seek Bibles and teachers of Christianity for their tribe. Their precise motives will never be known. Some Nez Perce assert that they had been led to believe that they would receive white men's goods as gifts if they accepted the teachings of "the Book of Heaven." More likely, they had been delegated by their headmen and chiefs to try to obtain Bibles and teachers for them as a means to increase their social importance and material wealth.

Two of the Nez Perce, Wé·ptes cɪmú·xcɪmux (Black Eagle) and Ká·ʔawapu· (Man Of The Dawn), contracted a white man's illness in St. Louis and died and were buried there. The other two started back west up the Missouri with Fontenelle in March 1832 on an American Fur Company steamboat. George Catlin, also a passenger on the vessel, painted their portraits in clothes some Sioux Indians had given them. Soon afterward, one of the two, Té·wɪs cɪʔcí·mnɪń (Horns Worn Out), died aboard the ship. The fourth, Heyú·xctohnɪń (Rabbit Skin Leggings), finally rejoined his band on the western Montana plains and was killed in a battle with the Blackfeets. He seems, however, to have informed the band members that white teachers with copies of "the book" would soon be coming to instruct them.

On their own, meanwhile, many Nez Perce headmen and chiefs were leading their bands in adopting some of the Christian practices that Spokan Garry had taught his audiences. Beginning in 1830 a cult showing pronounced Christian influences spread among the bands, and other Plateau tribes. American fur men, meeting groups of Nez Perce, were astounded by certain newly adopted practices that indicated a genuine Christian piety.

"Their ancient superstitions have given place to the more en-

In 1831 four Nez Perce went to St. Louis and asked for Bibles and teachers. Two of them died in St. Louis and the other two headed home the next year on a Missouri River steamboat. These portraits of Heýu·xctohniń (Rabbit Skin Leggings) and Té·wıs cıʔ cí·mnıń (Horns Worn Out) were painted aboard the boat by George Catlin. Courtesy Smithsonian American Art Museum, gift of Mrs. Joseph Harrison Jr.

lightened views of the christian faith, and they seem to have become deeply and profitably impressed with the great truth of the gospel," wrote Warren Ferris, a fur trapper. "They appear to be very devout and orderly, and never eat, drink, or sleep without giving thanks to God."

Capt. Benjamin L. E. Bonneville, a leader of American trappers, was surprised when some Nez Perce refused to join one of his hunting parties on a Sunday. It was a sacred day to them, they explained to him, "and the Great Spirit would be angry should they devote it to hunting." Unaware of the Red River Anglican origin of their teachings, Bonneville noted, "They even had a rude calendar of the fasts and festivals of the Romish Church, and some traces of its ceremonials. These have become blended with their own wild rites, and present a strange medley; civilized and barbarous. On the Sabbath, men, women and children array themselves in their best style, and assemble round a pole erected at the head of the camp. Here they go through a wild fantastic ceremonial; strongly resembling the religious dance of the Shaking Quakers. . . . During the intervals of the ceremony, the principal chiefs, who officiate as priests, instruct them in their duties, and exhort them to virtue and good deeds."

To many trappers, the Indians seemed ripe for Christianity. All that the Nez Perce had heard from the French Canadians and Iroquois and had seen around the fur company camps and posts was now reflected in the newly emerged cult. Nathaniel Wyeth, another American trader, repeatedly wrote in his journals of Nez Perce "praying, dancing & singing." Sunday there was a "parade of prayer . . . nothing is done Sunday in the way of trade with these Indians nor in playing games." On weekdays, while prayers were being said, "everyone ceases whatever vocation he is about if on horseback he dismounts and holds his horse on the spot until all is done." Prayers were common morning and evening, and a blessing was asked at every meal. The inspiration for the cult, which, as some suggest, may have been a more Christian-influenced revival of the pre-contact "prophet cult," was undoubtedly Garry. But the motives were secular, an attempt by headmen and others to acquire increased standing and success by sharing the seemingly more powerful supernatural ideas of the white men. "There is a new great man now getting up in the Camp and like the rest of the world he covers his designs under the cloak of religion," Wyeth noted on one occasion. "Perhaps ⅓ of the Camp follow him when he gets enough followers he will branch off and be an independent chief."

In the East, at the same time, news of the St. Louis visit of the four Nez Perce had been spread excitedly by the religious press, and various denominations began a race to respond to the Indians' "appeal" for missionaries. The first of them, a party of Methodists under Jason Lee, set off in 1834, traveling west with a fur traders' caravan. At the rendezvous, they raised the hopes of Nez Perce and Flatheads who thought that they would settle in their home villages as teachers. But Lee went on to the Willamette Valley in western Oregon and opened a mission for the Indians. The next year two more missionaries, Samuel Parker and Marcus Whitman, showed up at the 1835 rendezvous. They were sent by the American Board of Commissioners for Foreign Missions, representing Congregationalists, Presbyterians, and two smaller denominations.

Parker and Whitman found the Nez Perce enthusiastic and anxious to have them settle in their homelands and instruct their people. Whitman returned to the states for reinforcements, and Parker, a fifty-six-year-old New York preacher and former teacher at a girls' school, accompanied a Nez Perce band over the mountains to the Clearwater River. Intending to select a mission site and to return to meet Whitman and the reinforcements at the next year's rendezvous, Parker traveled through much of Nez Perce Country, finding the people generally hospitable and eager to participate in the prayers and singing of the religious services he conducted. He concluded that they were fit pupils for a missionary.

He selected several sites for a mission station, but he did not feel able to make the trip back across the mountains to the 1836 rendezvous in Wyoming. Giving a Nez Perce a note to take to Whitman, he went down the Snake and Columbia rivers and eventually returned to the East Coast by sea. At the rendezvous, in the Green River Valley in Wyoming, the Nez Perce gave a spirited welcome to Whitman, who returned with his newly married wife, Narcissa. Also with him were another missionary couple, Henry and Eliza Spalding, a helper named William H. Gray, and two Nez Perce boys, whom Whitman had taken east with him for instruction in English and whom he had named Richard and John. Though the Nez Perce were unaware of it, tension existed among the missionary party members. Spalding was a severe, thin-skinned Presbyterian of thirty-three with a bitterness that stemmed from a childhood knowledge that he had been born out of wedlock. Moreover, he had once proposed marriage to Narcissa, who had rejected him. Gray was an impatient fault-finder, anxious to be treated as an equal of the others.

Parker's optimistic note about the Nez Perce homeland cheered the missionaries, and they traveled on to Fort Walla Walla with a Hudson's Bay Company brigade that had come to the rendezvous and a large party of enthusiastic and helpful Nez Perce. Among the most eager to befriend the white men and women were the band's chief, Té·kıńıse wé·tes, whom Spalding later renamed Samuel, and a lesser headman named ʔá·lya?, which the American mountain men, partly in recognition of his ability in argument, had corrupted into The Lawyer. About forty years old and from the Kamiah region, Lawyer was the son of The Twisted Hair, who had met Lewis and Clark. He had taken his father's name, ʔá·lya?, though he was also known as Hallalhotsoot. On the plains, he had learned some English and, ambitious for prestige, had often interposed himself as interpreter and negotiator between the American fur men and the Nez Perce. Both he and Té·kıńıse wé·tes had been gravely wounded at the battle of Pierre's Hole during the rendezvous of 1832, when the Nez Perce had joined the mountain men against the Atsinas, and for the rest of his life Lawyer limped from his wound. Back home, he had been among those most influenced by Spokan Garry. He knew of the Nez Perce delegation to St. Louis and had looked forward to learning more from white teachers and their "book."

After reaching the Columbia River, the missionary families, thoroughly uncomfortable with each other, decided to establish separate missions. The Whitmans settled among the Cayuse Indians at Waiilatpu, "place of the rye grass," on the Walla Walla River in present-day southeastern Washington. The Spaldings, guided by Té·kıńıse wé·tes, selected a site among the Nez Perce about 3 kilometers (2 miles) above the mouth of Lapwai Creek. Near the village of a headman and shaman named Hınmató·tqakeykt (Thunder Eyes), Té·kıńıse wé·tes and other Nez Perce helped Gray and the Spaldings build a log house 13 x 5.4 meters (42 x 18 feet), divided by a partition into a living quarters and a classroom for the Indians. On December 23, 1836, the Spaldings moved into the building.

In the beginning, the missionary couple had good relations with most of the Nez Perce. Counseled by their headmen, the people willingly supplied food and labor to the Spaldings. They were excited by the novelty of having white teachers living among them and, fearful that they might find cause for leaving, did everything they could to help make them comfortable. They also were interested in the house and the material possessions and in everything the Spaldings taught them. They came in large numbers to Henry Spalding's morning and evening prayers and Sunday services. Aided by the translations of John, one of the Nez Perce boys whom Whitman had taken east and whom the Spaldings used as an interpreter, they learned to sing hymns and gospel tunes and followed intently Spalding's sermons and narrations of Bible stories, which he made more graphic to them by holding up pictures he had painted. Many Nez Perce became especially attached to Mrs. Spalding, a frail woman whose gentle nature contrasted with her husband's stern gruffness. She printed her own alphabet books to try to help the Nez Perce learn reading and writing, and she began a day school at the mission, attended principally by women, children, and a few of the important older men who hoped that what they learned would augment their status. Soon afterward, she also organized a class of Indian girls, instructing them in sewing and in the chores of running a white man's house.

Spalding, meanwhile, ingratiated himself to scores of Nez Perce who came to him every day for medical treatment for all sorts of ailments. Though he was unskilled as a physician, he drew on his stores of calomel and other medicines and taught bloodletting to his patients. Often, he sent Indians with medicines and instructions to patients in other villages or traveled to them himself. At the same time, anxious to end the Nez Perce annual migrations to the plains for buffalo and keep them settled around him the full year for his religious instruction, Spalding distributed seeds and some thirty hoes and began to teach them to plant gardens and orchards. By May 1, 1837, the Nez Perce had some 6 hectares (15 acres) of peas, potatoes, and garden vegetables under cultivation and had helped Spalding set out a nursery of apple trees.

Despite the good start, trouble gradually developed. Spalding had difficulty learning the Nez Perce language, and his temper ran short when individuals did not understand him or failed to follow his instructions. Believing himself a savior to people who had no religion and were misled by their shamans, whom he viewed as sorcerers, he had little tolerance for the Nez Perce cultural beliefs and habits and often erupted into bursts of anger at them. Some Nez Perce resented his hostility to some of their customs, including polygamy, sexual relationships between persons other than spouses of nuclear families, gambling, belief in guardian spirits, ceremonies accompanied by drumming, dancing, and singing, and other practices. And many took offense at the new ways of life that he tried to get them to adopt. Headmen and other males objected to doing manual labor and gardening, which they regarded as women's work. Others viewed agriculture as abhorrent and a desecration of their mother, the Earth. They ignored Spalding's efforts to get them to settle around the mission and resisted his insistence on attendance at prayer meetings and services. Still others found his teachings on Christian conduct and marriages and such concepts as their burden of original sin either incomprehensible or repugnant. Some headmen and shamans were angered by the missionaries' attempts to discredit them and wean their followers from them. And several, including Tackensuatis, perceiving that their expectations of material success and increased prestige were not being realized and that the Spaldings, unlike the American fur men on the plains, did not pay for them goods and services which the Nez Perce gave them, turned away from the missionaries.

The hot-tempered Spalding retaliated with punishments, withholding goods and favors, frightening individuals by consigning them to hell and eternal damnation, and threatening to whip them. When, by their silence, some headmen seemed to side with him against offenders, he carried out the threat, sometimes doing the whipping himself and sometimes persuading leading men to do so. Although such punishments contributed to a general waning of the Nez Perce initial enthusiasm for white teachers, the original motives for wanting them and the fear of losing them continued to be so strong that many headmen and their people remained protectively loyal to the Spaldings. Even some of those who turned away did so only temporarily.

In November 1837 Nez Perce women at the mission showed their affection for Mrs. Spalding when she gave birth to a baby girl whom she named Eliza. They helped Mrs. Spalding and treated both mother and daughter with a care and warmth that touched the missionaries.

The next year, Spalding strained the relationship by using threats and the whip to force Nez Perce males to help him relocate the mission to the mouth of Lapwai Creek on the site of present-day Spalding and the Nez Perce National Historical Park headquarters, an area he thought to be cooler and less bothered by mosquitoes. Though the Nez Perce objected to the forced labor and again smarted with resentments, they finally helped him build a new, two-story home and eventually a schoolhouse, blacksmith shop, and two small dwellings for assistants and Nez Perce schoolchildren.

That same year, William Gray, who had gone back to the states in 1837, returned with three more missionary families, the Asa B. Smiths, the Elkanah Walkers, and the Cushing Eellses. During their first winter, the newcomers stayed with the Whitmans at Waiilatpu, where they were joined by Lawyer, who taught Smith the Nez Perce language and Walker and Eells the Salish language. In the spring, the Walkers and Eellses erected a mission in the Spokans' country, and the Smiths, at Lawyer's urging, journeyed with him up the Clearwater River and established a mission for the Nez Perce a little northwest of present-day Kamiah, where Lewis and Clark had spent two months.

Despite the assistance given them by Lawyer, who used the white couple's reliance on him to swell his own prestige and authority, the Smiths' sojourn was not a happy one. Smith, who was twenty-nine, was well educated and more of a scholar than a minister. Both he and his wife, Sarah, were arrogant, had little respect for the Nez Perce, and held the other missionaries in contempt. They had been ordered to the Northwest by the American Board of Commissioners for Foreign Missions though they had wished instead to be sent to Siam. Smith nevertheless compiled considerable information about the Nez Perce, including a rough census that estimated their population at about three to four thousand. Furthermore, he reduced the Nez Perce language to writing and drew up the first Nez Perce dictionary and grammar. When a printing press reached Lapwai from missionaries in Hawaii, he criticized an eight-page primer in Nez Perce that Spalding produced on it and helped the older man turn out five hundred copies of a second volume, a twenty-page Nez Perce alphabet. Later,

Timothy was one of the first two converts to Christianity baptized by the Spaldings. Throughout his life Timothy remained loyal to the Spaldings and rescued their daughter Eliza when the Cayuses rose up against the Whitmans. Timothy was one of the few signers of the 1863 treaty whose lands were outside the new reservation's boundaries. Courtesy National Anthropological Archives, Smithsonian Institution (neg. no. 02923A).

Spalding also printed four books of the New Testament in the Nez Perce language, plus a copy of laws devised for the tribe. Smith had constant quarrels with Spalding and a number of conflicts with Kamiah area headmen. Eventually, he spent much of his time taking care of himself and his wife, who became sickly and complaining. Though the couple stayed two years at Kamiah, their missionary activities were minimal, and in April 1841 they closed the mission, went down the Columbia River, and left the Northwest by sea.

Spalding, meanwhile, made his first converts, baptizing two leading headmen who frequented the Lapwai mission though they came from other regions. One was Tamú·cın, a mild, sensitive man from Alpowa—the Sabbath observed—on the Snake River below the confluence with the Clearwater. Spalding called him Timothy. A devout Christian, he would also be a loyal, lifelong friend of the whites. The other was Tiwí·teqıs, who was the leader of the Nez Perce band in the present-day Wallowa Valley of northeastern Oregon and whom Spalding named Joseph. In the summer of 1839 Spalding accompanied Joseph on a visit to his Oregon homeland and became convinced of his genuine interest in Christianity. Spalding also baptized the children of Timothy and Joseph, including one of Joseph's sons who was born early in 1840 and whom the missionary named Ephraim. This was probably the future Chief Joseph.

Spalding's problems, however, had not eased. Mountain men, who had abandoned trapping and come to the Oregon Territory to seek permanent homes, appeared at the mission and vexed Spalding by taking the Indians' side in their quarrels with him. One of them, William Craig, who had married a daughter of Thunder Eyes, the Lapwai Creek shaman and headman whom Spalding called James, criticized Spalding's dictation to the Nez Perce and several times aroused his father-in-law against the missionary. At the same time, serious friction developed among the missionaries themselves, and they directed a stream of complaining letters about each other to the Mission Board in Boston. Dismayed, the Board in 1842 ordered the closing of both the Lapwai and Waiilatpu missions.

Henry Spalding Builds a Mission

Henry Spalding [*above*] and his wife, Eliza, originally planned to go as missionaries to the Osages in the upper Midwest. Marcus Whitman, however, prevailed on them to join him and his wife, Narcissa, in their work with the Nez Perce and other northwestern tribes. In November 1836 the Spaldings settled on Lapwai Creek, where they immediately built a structure that they used as a home and a church. The location they had chosen, however, was not the best, for it was plagued by mosquitoes. In the spring of 1838 they moved to the banks of the Clearwater, a more healthful location. Here they put up a number of buildings. Few traces of it remain, except for a pile of stones and the faint impression of the course of the mill race. In 1847, after the Whitmans were killed at their mission, Spalding and his family went to Oregon's Willamette Valley. There his wife died in 1851, and a few years later he married again. Spalding returned to Idaho in 1863 and worked with J. W. Anderson until 1864, when James O'Neil was appointed agent. Spalding continued his work in Idaho until his death in 1874. Spalding and his first wife are buried in the Lapwai Mission Cemetery at Spalding. Throughout his years with the Nez Perce, Spalding was a controversial character, for in his fervor to bring Christianity to the Nez Perce he demanded total obedience and acceptance of his ways. His rejection of those who did not accept Christianity created a split among the Nez Perce that was to plague them in the years to come.

The news shocked the missionaries. In an effort to undo the damage, Whitman rode to the East during the winter of 1842–43 and succeeded in having the board rescind its order. In his absence, however, significant developments occurred. The Whitmans were ill-suited as missionaries and had offended many Cayuses. Some of them had heard the Waiilatpu missionaries express hopes that white families beginning to arrive in the Northwest on the Oregon Trail would settle around the mission, and they were fearful that Whitman had gone to the East to get more whites who would take their lands. There was good reason for their fears, for Whitman actually did hope that he could bring back settlers who would live near him and help him "civilize" the Cayuses. Soon after his departure, at any rate, some Cayuses threatened Narcissa and burned the Waiilatpu gristmill.

News of the occurrences introduced Dr. Elijah White, newly arrived in the Willamette Valley as U.S. subagent to the Oregon Indians, to lead a party up the Columbia to investigate. Visiting both Waiilatpu and Lapwai, White decided to take steps to shore up the missionaries' authority over the Indians. Calling councils of the leading men at both places, he persuaded the two tribes to accept a set of laws which he had composed, probably with the advice of Spalding. They concerned such matters as murder, damaging property, and stealing.

White and Spalding thought the provisions dealt with all the principal offenses by the Indians which the missionaries had experienced. But the Indians would discover that the laws were both harsh and unjust and, while enforced against themselves, could not be made to apply to whites. At the same time, Spalding also complained of the loose governmental structure in which each band was autonomous. Without centralized, responsible tribal leadership, the laws could not be enforced, because headmen would continue to refuse to take responsibility for, or punish, wrongdoers whom they could claim were not members of their own band. To meet this problem, White directed the headmen of all the bands of each tribe, for the first time in their history, to choose a single "high chief of the tribe, and acknowledge him as such by universal consent."

The order, which contained the seed of continual discord, rivalry, and factionalism among the Indians, confused the Nez Perce, who were unable to settle on a choice. Under great pressure from White's party, however, they finally agreed to accept the subagent's candidate, Ellice, or, as Spalding spelled it, Ellis, the thirty-two-year-old grandson of the venerable war chief, Red Grizzly Bear. A product of the Red River school, Ellis spoke English, was a member of the pro-mission element in the tribe and friendly to Spalding, and had his own farm in the Kamiah region, as well as some sheep and cattle which he had gotten in trade at Hudson's Bay Company posts, and a herd of more than eleven hundred horses. After selecting twelve subchiefs, each with five police assistants, for the Nez Perce, and fastening a similar head-chief government on the Cayuses, White and his party returned to the Willamette Valley confident that they had strengthened the missionaries' position.

In the long run their hopes were doomed. Spalding had already created a rift among the Nez Perce between those who supported him and seemed to want to become Christians and those who ignored him or were actively hostile to him. The former he called "the Christian party" and the latter "the heathens." For a while after White's departure, he had an easier time. More Nez Perce participated in religious services and followed Spalding's sermons, and some 225 students, half of them adults, dutifully attended the mission school. About 100 students were "printing their own books with a pen." Spalding also reported that 140 Nez Perce had their own farms or were raising livestock, and that a number of women were learning to card, spin, weave, sew, and knit from Mrs. Spalding. Slowly a group of "civilized," or partly acculturated, Nez Perce was forming, and many of those learning the white man's skills and beliefs would never abandon them. But the new laws and head-chief government only deepened the rift Spalding had started. Though his opponents for a time let him alone, resentments smoldered and gradually increased. Ellis was a young man, with less standing than others, and most chiefs and headmen believed that he had no right to his position and ignored him. They refused to observe the laws or carry out punishments, and gradually enforcement broke down. In time, overt opposition to the missionaries surfaced again, and it became obvious that the head-men and their bands would not, or could not, adjust to giving up their autonomy and accepting a strange new form of government in which someone of lesser prestige and not of their own band would have missionary-directed authority over them. As friction broke out again, it appeared, moreover, that the Christian element, though de-terminedly loyal to the Spaldings, was in the minority.

Following Whitman's return in 1843, the missionaries' position continued to deteriorate. Whitman, accompanied by a thirteen-year-old nephew, Perrin Whitman, rode back across the plains with the first large emigration to Oregon, some one thousand settlers in covered wagons. Though the emigrants went on to the Willamette Valley, the Cayuses were sure that more would come and settle on their lands. Their unrest spread to the Nez Perce and other tribes and was quick-ened in 1844 by an event in California where a band of fifty promi-nent Nez Perce, Cayuse, Wallawalla, and Spokan chiefs had journeyed to trade horses and furs for cattle. At Sutter's Fort, the son of Pıyó·pıyo maqsmáqs, the leading Wallawalla headman who had relatives among the Nez Perce and Cayuses, was brutally murdered by a white man. The band hastened back to the Northwest without the cattle and demanded that Dr. White enforce his laws and bring the mur-derer to justice. The subagent could do nothing for them, and when he suddenly left Oregon to return to the East, many members of the affected tribes called for a war of revenge against all Americans. They were talked out of it by Dr. John McLoughlin, the British head of the Hudson's Bay Company in Oregon, whom they respected. But in 1846 another group from the same tribes returned to California intent on seeking out the murderer themselves. Before they could find their quarry, they were caught up in the turmoil of the Bear Flag Revolt and were enlisted by Gen. John C. Fremont as scouts in the conquest of California. During their return to the Northwest in 1847 some of them died from an epidemic of measles. By the time the survivors reached home, their anger against Americans had again reached a fever point.

At Lapwai and Waiilatpu, the missions were approaching a state of collapse. In 1845 Whitman had prevented the Cayuses from trying to intercept and turn back some of the settlers, and that year and the next large numbers of emigrants had streamed through Cayuse country. At both missions, wandering mixed-bloods and Delaware Indians from the East heightened the fears of many Nez Perce and Cayuses by telling them how other tribes had lost their lands and warning them that it was only a matter of time before they would suffer the same fate. Their tales inflamed their listeners, and at Lapwai Spalding faced new crises. Opponents openly taunted and harassed him, destroyed his mill dam, broke his meetinghouse windows, and even assaulted him physically. Those friendly to him became defensive, and their strength and influence waned. Gradually, many of them turned away from him and returned to their shamans and old ways. Others like Timothy remained loyal to the Spaldings but tended to avoid the mission.

At Waiilatpu, Whitman was faring even worse. Few Cayuses felt anything but hatred for him. To complicate matters for him, he was now facing competition from Catholic priests, who had settled in the Willamette Valley and were planning to open a mission among the Cayuses. The threat of such competition had hung over the Spaldings and Whitmans for a number of years. A few buffalo-hunting Nez Perce had come upon priests who were living with the Flatheads in Montana, and others of them, as well as Cayuses, had met priests at Fort Walla Walla. To the distress of Spalding and Whitman, some Indians had become converted to Catholicism. They had showed Spalding an anti-Protestant picture chart of a "tree" or "ladder," which the priests had used to instruct them. It had depicted the Protestants as the withered ends of the "true" Christian faith, falling into the flames of hell. Spalding, in anger, had retaliated by drawing a "Protestant tree," showing Martin Luther's path as the correct one.

The Catholic threat was almost the last straw for Whitman. He was disheartened by his lack of success, by the constant opposition of the Cayuses, and by a realization that some of them now wanted him to leave and give his place to the Catholics. Nevertheless, he stayed on, and in the fall welcomed a large, new emigration of settlers bound for the Willamette Valley. It was this group that spread the measles. The epidemic caught on quickly among the Cayuses and killed nearly half the tribe. Both Whitman and Spalding circulated among the people, administering medicine, but in the terror of the situation, a mixed-blood from Maine who had arrived with the emigrants, told some Cayuses that the missionaries were poisoning the Indians so that they could more quickly take their land.

The distraught Cayuses believed him, and on November 28, 1847, killed the Whitmans and eleven other whites at the mission. Three others died, unattended, of illness or while trying to escape, and forty-seven more, including the Spaldings' daughter Eliza, were taken captive. Spalding, who was returning to Waiilatpu from a Cayuse village, was warned and only barely escaped. After a harrowing trip, he got back to Lapwai to find his mission being looted by a crowd of angry young Nez Perce who had heard what had happened at Waiilatpu and sympathized with the Cayuses. He was rescued by a large number of his supporters and was taken to Craig's house, where he found his wife and other whites from the mission sheltered under the protection of the former mountain man's father-in-law, Thunder Eyes.

Although the Nez Perce headmen agreed not to risk a war with the Americans, they held the Spaldings and the other whites for almost a month as "hostages of peace" in Craig's home, telling Spalding that if American soldiers came up the Columbia to fight them, they could not protect the missionaries. Spalding's ordeal was finally ended by a party of Hudson's Bay Company men under a veteran trader, Peter Skene Ogden, who arrived at Fort Walla Walla on December 19 from the company's headquarters at Fort Vancouver. Ogden immediately opened negotiations with the Cayuses and Nez Perce and managed to ransom the prisoners from both Lapwai and Waiilatpu. Escorted by fifty Nez Perce, all of whom were still friendly to the missionaries, the whites from Lapwai arrived on January 1, 1848, at Fort Walla Walla, where the Spaldings were reunited with Eliza. The next day, Ogden started down the Columbia with the rescued prisoners. Three months later, the Walkers and Eellses, fearing for their own safety, finally left the Spokans. It was the end of the first Protestant missions.

Chapter Five
Time of Crises

The decade after the killing of the Whitmans was one of turbulence and tragedy for all tribes in the Northwest. Even if the bloodshed at Waiilatpu had not occurred, the subsequent course of history may not have differed greatly, for white settlers and miners, riding the tide of westering Manifest Destiny, poured into the Oregon Country, coveting tribal lands and realizing the Indians' worst fears. At the same time, the missionaries' activities and teachings had greatly weakened the ability of some of the strongest tribes, including the Nez Perce, to cope with the new situation, destroying their unity, undermining traditional authority and cultural sources of strength, and planting seeds of rivalry, doubt, and fear.

The Nez Perce, at the start of 1848, worried not only about settlers who would take their lands but American troops who would make war on them in revenge for what had happened to the missionaries. News that an army of Willamette Valley volunteers was on its way up the Columbia reached them from the Cayuses, who asked the Nez Perce and other tribes to join them in a war of defense. The Nez Perce were divided over what to do. Both Ellis, the white man's head chief, and Lawyer, the close friend of the missionaries, were in the buffalo-hunting country of Montana. In their absence, the other chiefs and headmen whom the Spaldings had won to Christianity, farming, and the observance of Dr. White's laws continued to argue against becoming involved in the Cayuses' troubles. The only way to protect their own people and their lands, they insisted, was to seek friendship with the Americans. Without unanimity, the headmen at length decided to watch events cautiously and, if possible, try to help bring peace.

The American volunteers reached the Cayuses' country in February and after driving off warriors built a post on the Whitman mission site. Hoping only to punish the murderers of the Whitmans and avoid stirring up other tribes in a general Indian war, the American leaders were concerned particularly about the intention of the Nez Perce, the largest and most powerful tribe in the area. Messages were sent to the Nez Perce asking them to come to a council. The invitation cheered the headmen who wished peace, and on March 6 some 250 Nez Perce, led by most of the chiefs who had been loyal to the Spaldings, arrived at the Americans' new post. With Joseph as their principal spokesman, Timothy, William Craig's father-in-law Thunder Eyes, a headman named Hími·n ʔilṗílp (Red Wolf) from Alpowa Creek, a man named Richard who had gone east with Whitman in 1835, and others convinced the Americans of their friendship and promised to try to get the Cayuses to hand over the murderers. That attempt proved unsuccessful, and the Nez Perce finally returned home with Craig, who had come over from his Lapwai Valley home to help at the Waiilatpu council and had there been appointed by the Americans as agent to the Nez Perce.

Impatient for action, the volunteers set off on their own to find the Cayuses, but they blundered into a battle with some Palouses, who forced them to retreat back to Waiilatpu. The Cayuses, meanwhile, dispersed for their safety, many of them going to live with Nez Perce friends and relatives. Their presence angered the peace-seeking headmen, who feared that the Americans would now accuse the Nez Perce of perfidy and make war on them. To forestall such a development, many headmen returned to Waiilatpu in May and complained to the Americans that the Cayuses were unwanted guests. They also said they had received word that Ellis and sixty members of his band had died on the buffalo plains of a sickness, which they thought was measles, and they asked the Americans to appoint a new head chief.

The Americans chose Richard, who was junior to all the other Nez Perce spokesmen present but who could converse in English and would be, in the Americans' opinion, the most pliable Nez Perce in their future dealings. To counter what must have been the surprised reaction of the older men, the Americans also named an official tribal war chief, bestowing the title on ʔapáswahayqt, a headman from present-day Asotin, Washington, whose father of the same name had met with Lewis and Clark and who himself had become one of the tribe's most respected hunting and war leaders. Because he wore a small trade mirror as a decoration, the whites called him Looking Glass. The appointment of Richard proved meaningless. No headman ever seems to have accepted him, and the Americans also paid him little or no attention. Though he is known to have continued as a member of the pro-American group until at least 1858, he failed so completely to fill the role of head chief that his appointment was soon forgotten.

After the Nez Perce left Waiilatpu, the Americans decided abruptly to search Nez Perce village for the Cayuses. At Red Wolf's village near the mouth of Alpowa Creek they were told that the Cayuses were farther east toward Lapwai. The Americans headed in that direction and, without opposition from the Nez Perce, who were too stunned to object to this first American invasion of their homeland, hurried from village to village along the Snake and Clearwater rivers. At Spalding's abandoned mission, the searchers learned that the Cayuse refugees had fled to the mountains.

The fruitless chase angered the volunteers. Shooting innocent Indians along the way, they returned to Waiilatpu, where a council of officers decided to end the pursuit. Announcing that the tribe had forfeited title to its lands in the Walla Walla Valley, the American commander, Lt. Col. James Waters, distributed land claims to fifty volunteers who offered to remain as a garrison for the post. The rest of the expedition returned to the Willamette Valley, hoping to induce more settlers to go to the Walla Walla. Few did so, and in time most of the volunteers returned to the Willamette. Until U.S. troops arrived in Oregon to establish authority in the eastern part of the territory, that region was deemed unsafe for white families. With the departure of Waters's force, an uneasy peace settled over the area, and the Nez Perce, Cayuses, Palouses, Wallawallas, Yakamas, and others who had been trying to evade the soldiers felt relieved. In 1850, five Cayuse leaders emerged from hiding and asked those whites who were still in the Walla Walla area for a conference. They were immediately seized and sent to Oregon City in the Willamette Valley, where they were tried, convicted, and hanged as the murderers of the Whitmans.

Lawyer, meanwhile, had returned from the buffalo country. He was not a chief but rather a camp crier who announced the day's activities and the headman's decisions to the people. He was ambitious and outgoing and, with his knowledge of English and skill at ingratiating himself with whites, was regarded by the other Nez Perce as a man whom the Americans liked and trusted. Lawyer artfully furthered this image among the other pro-white headmen. In August 1848 the Oregon Country (which two years before, south of the 49th Parallel, had become American) was declared a Territory, and in 1849, after his return from Montana, Lawyer learned that an American territorial governor, representing the "Great Chief in the East," had arrived in the Willamette Valley. Lawyer at once took a small party of chiefs to the Willamette to assure the new governor that the Nez Perce were friends. Gov. Joseph Lane flattered Lawyer and won his promise to enforce Dr. White's laws. Using his forceful personality, Lawyer gradually exerted more influence over the Christian and pro-white headmen. Grouping around him as a "Lawyer party," they let him advise them on their relations with the Americans and be their spokesman. Inevitably some Americans came to believe that he was the tribe's chosen headman or chief.

On their own initiative, Lawyer and the pro-white headmen zealously followed "the road of the whites," as the Spaldings had taught them to do. Convinced of the rightness of their new beliefs, they tended their farms and orchards, raised herds of cattle, and observed the laws and elements of Christianity. In the period of anxious peace, they promoted their course as offering the best hope of continuing safety from the Americans, and gradually, by example, preaching, and persuasion, swelled the pro-Christian group's numbers. Though the missionaries were no longer among them, the seeds the Spaldings had planted had not died. By the early 1850s American agents and other white visitors were reporting that many Nez Perce, especially in the Alpowa, Lapwai, and Kamiah areas, had gardens, orchards, and

ʔáꞏlyaʔ (The Lawyer) played a prominent role at the Treaty Council of 1855, assuring the Americans he was the spokesman for the Nez Perce Tribe. The Lawyer also signed the 1863 Treaty. Washington State Historical Society, Tacoma.

livestock and that a Christian-influenced cult—built on the Spaldings' teachings, but possibly reflecting also a revival of their own cult of the early 1830s—was widespread. Whole bands again assembled daily for morning and evening prayers and observed the Sabbath with services conducted in their own tongue by one of their own number. As the economic wealth of men like Lawyer and Timothy increased from their agricultural and pastoral activities, their political counsel, supported by William Craig, gained added stature, and their advice to follow the white men's laws and not to oppose a power that could destroy them even won acceptance by some headmen who had been anti-Christian and anti-American.

Yet the sharp division within the tribe remained. Many headmen and war chiefs like the doughty Looking Glass, Mitá·t wé·ptes (Three Feathers), and Tɪpɪyeléhne qá·ʔawpo (known to the whites as Eagle From The Light) ignored the Christian element and continued to follow their traditional beliefs and practices, to rely on their shamans and guardian spirits, and to cross the mountains to hunt buffalo and war on the Blackfeet, Sioux, and other enemies. They still distrusted the Americans and often met with headmen of other tribes—like Pɪyó·pɪyo maqsmáqs of the Wallawallas, Kamá·yaʔqɪn of the Yakamas, and Táwɪtoy, or The Young Chief, of the Cayuses of the Umatilla Valley—who also believed that soon the Americans again would try to take their lands.

West of the Cascades, meanwhile, the white population was increasing, and in 1853 Washington Territory was created. In the National Capital, Isaac I. Stevens, a thirty-five-year-old, politically ambitious veteran of the Mexican War, was appointed governor and Superintendent of Indian Affairs for the new territory and was simultaneously given charge of the most northerly of four survey groups of civilians and military men being sent by the War Department to find the most feasible route across the trans-Mississippi West for a railroad to the Pacific. Stevens was energetic and dynamic and saw his three jobs complementing each other toward a single end that would advance his career. As governor, he would gain national prominence, he hoped, by building up the population and prosperity of the new territory. That meant, in his opinion, finding a railroad route that Congress would accept as less expensive and more feasible than any farther south and that could be used to lure settlers to the territory and link their commerce with that of the rest of the nation. As Superintendent of Indian Affairs, he would be in a position to clear Indians from the route of his railroad, as well as from lands needed by new settlers.

Stevens started west with his main survey group from St. Paul, Minnesota, but directed another party under Capt. George B. McClellan, the future Civil War general, to explore in an eastward direction from the Pacific Coast and find a pass over the Cascade Mountains for a rail line. By the summer of 1853, McClellan and his men were in the Yakamas' country, and other military and civilian groups, as well as individuals, on Stevens's survey business were crisscrossing the lands of the Palouses, Nez Perce, and other tribes. All of the tribes wondered what they were doing and became alarmed when some Yakamas, who were assisting McClellan's men, were told that next year a Great Chief (Stevens) would buy the Indians' lands in a treaty meeting and open them to white settlers.

The Nez Perce were again filled with anxiety, which was not allayed when, on several occasions, members of Stevens's expedition suddenly appeared in their villages, having crossed the Bitterroots by both the Lolo Trail, which Lewis and Clark had taken, and the southern trail, which ran from the upper Bitterroot Valley in Montana to the South Fork of the Clearwater River and over which the Nez Perce had once brought Samuel Parker. Stevens himself crossed the mountains north of the Nez Perce lands, but on his way to Fort Walla Walla and the lower Columbia, he met many Nez Perce. Though he said nothing about wanting the Indians' lands and soon proceeded with all his men to Puget Sound, most Nez Perce headmen were sure that the danger of war had again arisen.

They were not wrong. Stevens had found a feasible railroad route, and in 1854 he returned to Washington DC by sea and secured permission to make treaties with the northwestern tribes, as well as the Blackfeet on the northern plains, where he wanted to bring intertribal peace to safeguard the railroad. Sectional interests, building up between the North and the South in the capital, held up a decision on the railroad, but Stevens believed the delay was temporary. He returned to Olympia, the capital of the new territory, and in January and February 1855 swept through western Washington, forcing headmen of the tribes west of the Cascades by threats and trickery to sign away their lands and accept small reservations.

Word of what was happening heightened the alarm east of the Cascades. Before the bands could agree on what to do, two emissaries from Stevens came upriver in April and, visiting each tribe, persuaded their headmen to meet with Stevens and Joel Palmer, the Superintendent of Indian Affairs in Oregon, in the latter part of May at Mill Creek, some ten kilometers (six miles) above Waiilatpu in the Walla Walla Valley. Looking Glass and several of the anti-white headmen and chiefs were in Montana, hunting buffalo. In their absence, the Christians and other Nez Perce headmen, deciding that they had no choice but to hear what Stevens had to say, agreed to let Lawyer be their spokesman, hoping that he could avert any attempt to take their lands.

The council lasted from May 29 to June 11, 1855, and was the largest ever held in the Northwest. Several thousand Indians were present, including most of the Nez Perce nation, Wallawallas, Cayuses, Umatillas, Yakamas, and representatives of a number of other tribes. To win compliance from the Indians, Stevens sent keelboats up the Columbia ahead of him loaded with presents and food, and throughout the council, he feasted the important men.

From reports from his agents and from priests who had been with some tribes, Stevens expected trouble from Pıyó·pıyo maqsmáqs, Kamá·ya?qın, Young Chief, and a few others whom he termed "malcontents," and he brought along a military escort of forty-seven soldiers. But he also understood that the large and powerful Nez Perce delegation was friendly, and he looked to them for support. Their arrival on May 24, with Lawyer—who carried an American flag—and the chiefs and Craig at their head, was bold and stirring; riding at a gallop, they circled the reviewing Americans at the flagpole on the council grounds and put on a series of exciting equestrian displays and a war dance. Stevens warmly welcomed Lawyer as head chief of the tribe. Neither Lawyer nor Craig corrected him, possibly believing, as did the headmen, that the Americans were officially appointing Lawyer as their new head chief. From then on, Lawyer formally asserted title to that position, though he did not have the prestige or authority that Stevens thought he had. The individual headmen and chiefs continued to regard their bands as autonomous. The anti-Americans even ignored him, and neither they nor Lawyer assumed that he could speak for them unless they asked him to do so.

With Craig and several others acting as interpreters, the council got off to a bad start for Stevens and Palmer. The interpreting was poor. Even so, the Indians understood enough to recognize that the Americans were treating them patronizingly and with dishonesty. They knew what the Americans wanted, but for several days Stevens and Palmer beat all about the bush, thanking the tribes for their friendship to whites, relating falsely that the American Government had made the Cherokees and other Southeastern tribes prosperous and happy by moving them from their countries to new lands west of the Mississippi, out of the way of "bad" whites, and going into a long, rambling, and distorted lesson on Indian-white history since the time of Columbus. They reverted repeatedly to a list of things the Americans wanted to give to the assembled tribes: schools, blacksmith shops, carpenters, farmers, plows, wagons, sawmills, gristmills, blankets, cloth, bake ovens, tin kettles, frying pans, and teachers who would help them learn to make clothes and become farmers, mechanics, doctors, and lawyers. Only once did Stevens briefly allude to the real purpose of the council, stating, "Now we want you . . . to have your tract with all these things; the rest to be the Great Father's for his white children."

The single allusion was enough. The Indians could see that the Americans were masking their real purpose. Besides, the northwestern tribes knew the real story of the ousting of the Southeastern Indians from their homes; for fifteen years, Delawares, mixed-bloods, and others from the East had been telling them of the brutal "Trail

The Council of 1855

Isaac Stevens was an ambitious man
who believed he could convince
the northwestern tribes to move
onto reservations so that the Federal
Government could build a railroad
and the settlers could move onto
the rich agricultural lands of the
Columbia Plateau. To do this he
called a council of all tribes east of the
Cascades to meet in the Walla Walla
Valley in the spring of 1855. The tribes
were aware that Stevens wanted to establish reservations and were angered
by his failure to be frank with them.
Finally he outlined his proposals and
day after day hammered away at the
tribes' protests. Even the unexpected
arrival of Looking Glass, who opposed
the idea of a reservation, did not sway
Stevens from his path. In the end the
tribes agreed to the treaties Stevens
had proposed, yet within months
almost all were at war except for the
Nez Perce and a few other tribes. The
drawing of the Nez Perce arriving at
the council was done by Gustavus
Sohon, at that time a private in the
U.S. Army.

of Tears" endured by the Cherokees. The headmen, angered by the Americans' glibness and crooked talk, were restless. "You have spoken in a round about way," Pıyó·pıyo maqsmáqs told Stevens. "Speak straight. I have ears to hear you. . . . Speak plain to us."

Anger also erupted over a suspicion among some chiefs that Stevens was playing secretly on Lawyer, getting him to approve the selling of the Nez Perce' lands so the Americans could then bring pressure on other tribes. One night, according to a story that Lawyer later told, he went to Stevens's tent and, informing him of a plot being hatched among the Cayuses, Yakamas, and Wallawallas to massacre the governor, announced that he wished to move into Stevens's camp to show the plotters that the Americans were "under the protection of the head chief of the Nez Perce." There is no record of such a plot or occurrence. Some Nez Perce, however, have claimed that suspicion was running so high against Lawyer's collusion with the Americans, even among his own people, that he moved temporarily to Stevens's camp for his own safety.

On June 4 Stevens finally revealed his plan to establish two reservations, one in Nez Perce Country for the Nez Perce, Cayuses, Wallawallas, Umatillas, and Spokans, and the other in Yakama country for the Yakamas and all the many tribes and bands along the Columbia River from the Dalles to the Okanogan and Colville valleys in northeastern Washington. The Indians would sell the rest of the country, including the areas through which the projected railroad would be built. He spent two days explaining the reservations and tracing their boundaries on a map, but he made little headway. Save for Lawyer and a few of the Nez Perce headmen whose territories were unaffected, the Indians reacted coldly.

As the days passed, Stevens became impatient. He worked harder on Lawyer, promising him personal benefits and payments befitting his position as head chief. With the help of Timothy and others, Lawyer pressured the other headmen and chiefs, showing them that the only territory the Nez Perce would have to sell were border areas where none of their villages were located and arguing that under the treaty the Americans would protect their villages and lands from whites, who would not be allowed on the reservation. If they turned down the treaty, Lawyer warned them, there would be no protection. Whites would seize their lands anyway, and there would be war. Finally, all the headmen and chiefs agreed to go along with the treaty. The news cheered Stevens, but the tribes that were giving up their homelands, particularly the Cayuses and Wallawallas, were dismayed by the Nez Perce decision and continued to resist. In an effort to hurry the council to a close, Stevens made a sudden series of new offers, proposing a third reservation for the Cayuses, Wallawallas, and Umatillas centered in Oregon's Umatilla valley and various payments, gifts, and services to the tribal headmen, who included two of his principal opponents, Pıyó·pıyo maqsmáqs and Young Chief. Moreover, he announced that no tribe would have to go on the new reservations until the President and the Senate approved the treaties and the promised homes, blacksmith shops, and other buildings were constructed.

The new offers had an effect, and Stevens gradually wore down the headmen's resistance. Though it appears that the terms were still not clear to them, and that some still opposed the treaties, they all reluctantly agreed to sign. Joseph made a final plea that the Americans be sure that his Wallowa homeland in Oregon be included in the Nez Perce reservation, and Red Wolf asked that Craig be allowed to stay with the Nez Perce "because he understands us." Stevens reassured Joseph and agreed to Red Wolf's request, thus confirming Craig's right to a claim he had filed for his Lapwai Valley home and 259 hectares (640 acres, later found to be 630) under the 1850 Oregon Donation Land Law. It made Craig the first permanent white settler in the present state of Idaho.

The council ended in a dramatic climax. Looking Glass had learned of the meeting and, crossing hurriedly from Montana, reached the conference just before the signing. His arrival with three of the tribe's elderly and most notable buffalo-hunting chiefs and a retinue of about twenty warriors, all in buffalo robes and painted for war with one of the warriors carrying a staff from which dangled a Blackfoot scalp, threw the council into a commotion and threatened to undo everything Stevens had won. "My people," Looking Glass scolded the Nez Perce, "what have you done? While I was gone, you have sold my country. . . . Go home to your lodges. I will talk to you."

That night, he heaped scorn on the headmen who had agreed to sign, and the next day the seventy-year-old war chief took over from Lawyer as spokesman. "It was my children who spoke yesterday," he told the Americans, "and now I have come." He ran his finger along Stevens's map of the new reservation, outlining the borders of all the Nez Perce' lands as they had traditionally existed. *That* was the reservation he wanted. Stevens and Palmer argued with him, but got nowhere, and Stevens finally adjourned the session, telling him to think the matter over and talk to the other Nez Perce. After the meeting, Stevens privately reassured Lawyer that the next day he would recognize only Lawyer as the head chief and would not let Looking Glass speak. The Nez Perce, he told Lawyer, had given him their word and could not break it.

In a stormy session in the Nez Perce camp that night, Lawyer convinced the headmen that there would be trouble if they broke their pledge. A majority of those present finally reaffirmed their acceptance of the Americans' appointment of Lawyer as the head chief, and Looking Glass and the other elderly chiefs who had come with him, recognizing that their respective bands would lose none of their lands, at length gave their assent to the treaty. The triumph increased Lawyer's prestige among the pro-Christian headmen but did nothing to moderate the feelings of the anti-Americans. Even some of those like Joseph, who wanted peace, were doubtful about the course they had accepted and feared that Looking Glass would be proven right. The next day, Lawyer signed the treaty. He was followed by Looking Glass and Joseph, who made their marks in silence. The other Nez Perce chiefs and headmen—fifty-six in all—added their marks, and then the Cayuses signed their treaty. All the other tribes had already signed, and the council was ended.

Though each Nez Perce chief or headman signed only for his own band or village, satisfied that he had not sold any of his ancestral

When the Treaty Council of 1855 began, ʔapáswahayqt (Looking Glass) was in Montana hunting buffalo. His dramatic arrival near the end of the sessions momentarily threw the outcome into doubt. Looking Glass's son, also called Looking Glass, was an important figure in the 1877 War. Courtesy Washington State Historical Society, Tacoma.

lands, the Nez Perce treaty from the Americans' point of view established a reservation of about 13,000 square kilometers (5,000 square miles) for the entire Nez Perce tribe, which they assumed was now led by Lawyer. Since the leaders of every band had signed, the treaty eventually became in the eyes of the Nez Perce the basic document in their dealings with the American government. From its agreements and conditions stemmed—and still stem—the fundamental rights of the Nez Perce and the obligations of the Federal Government to them, for never again did the United States make a treaty with the tribe in which all the bands were present and able to speak for themselves.

The Nez Perce relinquished little land which they regarded as their own: a narrow strip of mountainous hunting grounds in the south running across the center of present-day Idaho and a grazing area on both sides of the Snake River west of the mouth of Alpowa Creek in present-day Washington. In 1957 the Indian Claims Commission determined that they had also ceded a long strip of the mountains and forests on their eastern border, comprising principally the drainages of the upper North Fork of the Clearwater, the Lochsa and Selway rivers, and a part of the Salmon River. For what they sold, the headmen were promised two schools, two blacksmith shops, a sawmill, a flour mill, a hospital, and other facilities, all of which would be built for them within one year of ratification of the treaty by the Senate; an agent, two teachers, and ten persons to maintain the buildings for twenty years; and $200,000, payable in graduated amounts annually over twenty years, for improvements and for blankets, clothing, and other goods and services. The tribe's head chief would receive a house and an annual salary of $500 a year for twenty years.

No whites, other than those in government service for the Indians, would be allowed on the reservation without the consent of the tribal leaders and the agent. The idea of having the Spokans move onto the reservation with the Nez Perce was abandoned. Stevens would meet with that tribe and make other arrangements. The Nez Perce retained the right to hunt, fish, dig roots, and gather berries on the lands they had ceded and to pasture their livestock on any land adjoining the reservation not owned by whites. Finally, before leaving the council grounds, Stevens appointed William H. Tappan, one of his assistants at the council, as the new agent for the Nez Perce, with Craig as his interpreter.

The tribes were told that they would not have to withdraw from the lands they sold until one year after the government ratified the treaties. Nevertheless, Stevens and Palmer immediately sent word to the newspapers in western Oregon and Washington that the ceded areas were open for settlement. Inevitably, that would lead to trouble. Stevens then traveled from the Walla Walla to Montana to meet with the Blackfeet. On the way, he concluded a treaty with the Flatheads, Kutenais, and Pend d'Oreilles, inducing them against their will to go onto a single reservation and cede lands for his railroad. He wanted delegates from the western tribes to join him in his meeting with the Blackfeet to solemnize a peace pact between them, and he had invited Lawyer. The head chief's old wound was hurting him, however, and Looking Glass, as second in rank to Lawyer, was prevailed on to lead the Nez Perce delegation. Before Stevens left the Flatheads, Tappan, Craig, and Looking Glass joined him with many Nez Perce chiefs, including Eagle From The Light, Three Feathers, White Bird from Salmon River, and a supporter of Lawyer, whom Spalding had named Jason. Together with a party of Flatheads, Kutenais, and Pend d'Oreilles, they participated in the council with the Blackfeet, and Stevens had the satisfaction of bringing about a peace that, despite occasional clashes, endured thereafter between the longstanding enemies.

On his way back to Puget Sound, Stevens received the stunning news that warfare had erupted both east and west of the Cascades with many tribes that had signed treaties with him. The entire Northwest was inflamed, reported the messenger, whom a Nez Perce had guided across the Lolo Trail. East of the Cascades, miners and land-hunters, responding to Stevens's announcement, had come onto the lands of the Yakamas and other tribes. Gold had been discovered in the Colville Valley, and the resultant rush led to conflicts with Indians who had felt all along they should not have signed the treaties. Several whites, including the Yakamas' agent, had been killed, and Federal troops stationed at The Dalles had marched into the Yakamas' country. The Indians had halted them, however, and forced them to retreat with casualties. As alarm had spread among the whites, another Federal force was preparing to launch a punitive expedition against the Yakamas.

At almost the same time, conflicts had broken out between whites and Indians in southwestern Oregon and in western Washington, where Stevens had earlier dragooned the tribes into selling their lands. The territorial leaders of both Oregon and Washington had raised companies of volunteers to cope with what appeared to be a concerted Indian uprising throughout the Northwest. Even in the Walla Walla area, the Cayuses, Wallawallas, and Palouses were rumored to have joined the Yakamas in the fighting, which many whites thought was directed by Kamá·ya?qın and Pıyó·pıyo maqsmáqs. No one knew where the Nez Perce stood, the courier told Stevens.

Looking Glass and his Nez Perce delegation were still with Stevens and, though inwardly sympathetic to the warring tribes, agreed among themselves to take him under their protection until they got back home and could decide with the other band leaders what the Nez Perce should do. The party passed through the countries of the Coeur d'Alenes and Spokans and found both divided over whether to join the war. In councils with their headmen, Stevens threatened them all with stern punishment if they entered the conflict, but he received a dressing-down from Spokan Garry, the educated Christian, who made it clear that the war had been caused by Stevens's threats and pressures that had forced the headmen to sell their peoples' lands. "If you take those Indians for men, treat them so now," Garry admonished the American. "The Indians are proud, they are not poor. If you talk truth to the Indians to make a peace, the Indians will do the same for you."

Stevens was nettled, and he was now worried about the disposition of the Nez Perce. With Looking Glass's escort, he hurried to the Clearwater and at Lapwai found Lawyer assembled with a large number of pro-peace Nez Perce, who offered more than 200 warriors to see him safely through the countries of the Cayuses and Wallawallas. A council was held, in which all the Nez Perce pledged friendship to the Americans. It was deceptive, because it concealed a deep division among the bands. They had been under great pressure from emissaries from the warring tribes, and many headmen and chiefs, seeing the justice of the war, had come close to joining it. But a council of all the bands had been held, and Lawyer had reminded them that they had done well at the Walla Walla council and that if they went to war, their own people faced misery and death from retaliating Americans. Even the most belligerent headmen and war chiefs were pulled up short by Joseph's argument that he wanted no American troops in his homeland. In the end, the council decided to do what was necessary to preserve the people's security, even though the hearts of some of those who voted with Lawyer were with the embattled tribes and they refused to participate with the Lawyer group in giving any further help to the Americans.

Stevens appreciated Lawyer's offer of an escort, but it proved unnecessary. A messenger arrived with word that Oregon volunteers had just defeated a large group of Palouses, Wallawallas, and Cayuses in a four-day battle north of the Walla Walla River and had killed Pıyó·pıyo maqsmáqs, seizing him when he had come into their camp under a white flag of truce for a parley, and scattered the Indians. The news strengthened Lawyer's hand, and he persuaded Stevens to let a "guard of honor" of sixty-nine Nez Perce headed by Tıpıyeléhne tí·menın (Spotted Eagle) accompany him to the Walla Walla Valley. Near Waiilatpu, Stevens joined the Oregon volunteers and learned that another force of regulars and volunteers had also defeated a group of Yakamas.

The fighting, however, was far from ended. Though beaten in battle, the tribes east of the Cascades were still unconquered and were determined to resist the invasion of their homelands. But west of the Cascades, where the tribes had driven the settlers into blockhouses, Stevens considered the situation more urgent. Thanking the Nez Perce, he hurried on to Olympia, and for the next few months directed a campaign that finally crushed the Puget Sound tribes. Meanwhile the Oregon volunteers and newly formed units of Washington militia warred ruthlessly on any Indians they could find. They shot down innocent groups and lone individuals, hanged one Nez Perce man whom they suspected of spying on them, made inconclusive forays into the Palouse and Yakama countries, drove off the cattle of non-combatant Indians, and finally massacred a peaceful camp of Cayuse and Wallawalla women, children, and old men near present-day Elgin in Oregon's Grande Ronde Valley, on the border of Joseph's Wallowa homeland.

The whites' provocations, particularly the hanging of the Nez Perce, strained the collective patience of the Nez Perce chiefs and headmen. Again and again, the rise of war fever tested the persuasive powers of Lawyer, Timothy, Spotted Eagle, Jason, and others. But the peace leaders clung to their conviction that the Nez Perce safety depended on their faithful adherence to the pledges given Stevens and, aided by Craig, they managed each time to restrain the anger of such men as Looking Glass, Three Feathers, and Eagle From The Light, who argued heatedly that Stevens's treaty was a fraud designed to deceive the Indians.

Even as the tribe polarized into bitter pro-treaty and anti-treaty factions, the Lawyer group continued to try to convince the Americans that the Nez Perce were their true friends. Forty-seven of the Lawyer group enrolled officially as a "Company M" in the Washington Territorial Volunteers and campaigned with the whites for a time through the Palouse and Yakama countries. On other occasions, Lawyer's followers sold horses to the Americans (for which the tribe was still asking payment as late as 1877) and provided escorts to American supply and ammunition trains. Captain John, a pro-Lawyer headman from a Snake River village south of present-day Lewiston, was actually responsible for the events leading to the Grande Ronde Valley massacre. After leading the Americans to the hidden camp, he was sent forward to ask for a parley, but he returned claiming that the people were hostile to him. The volunteers then charged and showed the terror-stricken Indians no mercy.

At times, Lawyer almost lost control. Joseph and Red Wolf, among others, had now abandoned their faith in the Americans and were giving up their interest in Christianity and Spalding's teachings. The Nez Perce fury rose so high, even at Lapwai, that Craig was prepared to flee. The tension was finally abated by the intercession of the regular army, whose leaders accused the volunteers of prolonging the hostilities by their reckless actions. With troops of the 9th U.S. Infantry, Col. George H. Wright, in May and June 1856, restored peace among the Yakamas, then sent a force under Lt. Col. Edward J. Steptoe to accompany Stevens to a new council that Stevens called with the tribes in the Walla Walla Valley. There was bad blood between Stevens and the regular officers, for the Indians had convinced the latter that Stevens's treaties and highhanded conduct at the first Walla Walla council had caused the war and that he and the volunteers were now trying to drive them from their lands even before the treaties were ratified.

At Walla Walla, Stevens hoped to get the Indians to admit that they had accepted the treaties and had then broken them while he was with the Blackfeet. Instead, he was greeted at the September meeting with hostility and contempt. A large number of both Nez Perce factions appeared and took opposite sides. After Timothy and Thunder Eyes, now known to the whites as James, assured Stevens that the Nez Perce would stand by the treaty, Joseph, Red Wolf, Eagle From The Light, and a chief named Speaking Owl all rose to say that they had not understood the treaty, that they had no intention of giving away any land, and that Lawyer had sold it unfairly.

Stevens finally ended the council and, escorted by the Washington volunteers and a band of 50 pro-treaty Indians led by Spotted Eagle, set off for The Dalles. As they started to move, they were attacked by angry Indians from many tribes, including some 120 of the anti-treaty Nez Perce. For a while, Nez Perce faced each other in the skirmish. Finally, Steptoe rescued Stevens and went down the Columbia with him. The episode induced Wright to go to the Walla Walla area in October and meet with the Indians. Few of them responded to the call for a new conference—only two Nez Perce headmen showed up—but Wright assured them that he understood their grievances against Stevens and that, until the treaties were ratified, he would keep all unauthorized whites out of their lands. With the troublemaking volunteers gone, he had Steptoe issue a proclamation barring the country east of the Cascades to all whites save missionaries, Hudson's Bay Company employees, and prospectors traveling to the northern mines. To enforce the peace, Steptoe built a permanent post on Mill Creek, which eventually grew into the present city of Walla Walla.

The peace was more of an armed truce and lasted less than two years, from October 1856 until May 1858. Though Stevens, who went to Washington in 1857 as territorial delegate to Congress, pleaded for the treaties, the Senate did not ratify them until April 1859, four years after the council. (When the Civil War came, Stevens entered it as a Union officer and was killed in 1862, at the age of forty-four, in the Battle of Chantilly.) In the Northwest the pro-treaty Indians waited restlessly for their promised payments and services while their anti-treaty opponents scoffed and jeered at them, saying that they would never get them. Meanwhile large numbers of whites, many of them miners on their way to and from the Colville Valley gold mines, continued to enter the lands of the Yakamas, Palouses, Spokans, Coeur d'Alenes, and other northern tribes. The rough-hewn California miners thought nothing of pillaging and killing Indians. The Indians retaliated and, despite the presence of the military, the murders of Indians and whites increased. A new tension also developed from the government's decision to build a wagon road from Fort Benton to the site of old Fort Walla Walla on the Columbia River. It would pass directly through the lands of the Coeur d'Alenes and others. Word of it raised new alarms, even around Steptoe's post at Walla Walla.

In May 1858 Steptoe set out for the north with 150 soldiers and two howitzers to try to check the unrest. Timothy and some of his people helped ferry the command across the Snake River at Alpowa and then joined the expedition. Near present-day Rosalia, Washington, the column was attacked and surrounded on a high hill by a large body of Coeur d'Alenes, Palouses, Spokans, and Yakamas, who thought the troops had come to make war on them. The troops escaped during the night and retreated in disorder to the Snake, where Timothy's people ferried them back to safety. During the fighting, Steptoe sent a messenger to Lawyer, and the head chief and more than 200 Nez Perce warriors now met the bedraggled troops and accompanied them back to their fort.

The rout of the regulars proved to be the final undoing of all the tribes save the Nez Perce. In retaliation, a determined army swept through the Yakamas' country, killing many people, scattering the bands, and breaking the last trace of power of the Yakamas and allied tribes of the Columbia River. Colonel Wright led another force to Fort Walla Walla and, meeting with Lawyer and chiefs of his faction, bound them to his side with a new treaty of friendship, which required them to aid the United States in his war against other tribes and promised them arms for their defense. Twenty-one Nez Perce signed the compact, after which Wright formed a unit of thirty Nez Perce scouts, put them in the blue uniforms of the regular army, and placed them under the command of Lt. John Mullan. The force of seven hundred men then set out, with the Nez Perce to be employed as a formal regular army unit riding in the advance.

In a stern, whirlwind campaign, Wright shattered a combined force of Spokans, Coeur d'Alenes, Palouses, and a few Yakamas at two battles near the present city of Spokane on September 1 and 5, 1858. The Nez Perce scouted and skirmished for the Americans at both battles, and Mullan cited one chief, Yu·cınmé·lıxkın from Kamiah, for particular bravery. The Yakama chief, Kamá·ya?qın, was wounded and escaped to Canada. The other surviving leaders appealed for peace, but Wright hanged some of them and then scoured their countries, seizing others on the slightest pretext and hanging them, too.

By October 5 Wright was back at Fort Walla Walla, having broken forever the military power of all the tribes he had beaten. A permanent peace was established on the lands that Stevens had tried to clear of Indians, but the Nez Perce would never forget how the Americans had hanged the chiefs who had surrendered. On October 31, although the Senate had still not ratified the treaties, the Walla Walla Valley was finally deemed safe and was formally opened to white settlement.

By the following April, some two thousand whites had poured into the valley and begun to spread across eastern Washington. When the treaties were ratified, the defeated tribes went quietly onto their reservations, and their ceded lands, too, passed into white ownership. The Nez Perce had so far safeguarded their country, but they were now alone—and divided.

Chapter Six
The Gathering Storm

On July 22, 1859, a new agent, A. J. Cain, informed Lawyer and many headmen of both factions that the treaty they had made with Stevens in 1855 had finally been ratified and that they could now feel secure on their lands within the reservation boundaries. Despite his assurances, the Nez Perce lands were anything but secure. West of the reservation line the country was filling with land-hungry settlers and miners restless with rumors that the Bitterroot Mountains on the eastern side of the reservation were rich in minerals.

One adventurer, Elias D. Pierce, who had been in the California gold rush and had been trading intermittently with the Nez Perce since 1852, had settled at the bustling new town of Walla Walla and, in 1858 and 1859, had visited Indian villages along the Clearwater and panned a little gold. At the time, he considered it too dangerous to pursue his quest, but early in 1860 he and a companion, Seth Ferrell, returned to the village of a friendly, pro-Lawyer headman near the mouth of the Clearwater's north fork, where Lewis and Clark had built their canoes in 1805. On February 20, a little higher up on the Clearwater, they found enough gold to induce them to go back to Walla Walla for equipment and supplies. Cain, who was based there, learned of their plans and warned them to stay off the Nez Perce reservation. Ferrell dropped out, but Pierce brushed off the warning and with three other men returned to the Clearwater, where they were accosted by Lawyer and a number of his headmen, who questioned them about their intentions and then, seeing that they were not settlers after their lands, agreed to let them prospect. Some of Cain's authorities appeared however, and once more Pierce returned to Walla Walla, this time to raise a party too large for the agent to stop.

After telling Cain falsely that he would prospect outside the reservation's eastern boundary and would get there by a northern route that did not cross the reservation, Pierce started off again in August with ten men. Stealing onto the reservation, he ferried the Snake River at Timothy's village at Alpowa and made his way to the upper north fork of the Clearwater, guided through the mountainous country, according to one story by Timothy's nineteen-year-old daughter, Jane, who was married to the interpreter at Fort Walla Walla. On September 30 one of his men, W. F. Bassett, made a rich strike on Canal Gulch, a headwater of Oro Fino Creek, on the northern part of the reservation.

The news was carried back to Walla Walla, and in December, before winter snows closed in the mountain, a group of forty prospectors reached Canal Gulch and began a settlement, which they named Pierce. With the coming of spring, Cain knew, more prospectors would be invading the reservation than either he or the army could contain. After discussions with his superiors, Cain concluded that to avoid a war he would have to get the Nez Perce to agree to amend the 1855 treaty, giving the prospectors the right of access to, and use of, the mining district. In April 1861, accompanied by Edward R. Geary, the superintendent of Indian Affairs for Oregon and Washington, he met with Lawyer and a large group of his followers at Lapwai.

His task was easier than he expected. By then the frenzied rush of miners was underway. Since early February gold had been coming into Walla Walla from the mines, spreading excitement throughout the Northwest. In violation of the 1855 treaty, almost a thousand miners were already on the northern part of the reservation, with thousands more on their way. More settlements were springing up on the Indians' lands and merchants, adventurers, and camp followers were pouring in to set up canvas-walled shops and saloons. Though some whites ran into groups of Nez Perce who angrily tried to bar their way, the Indians' opposition was ineffective and was usually ended quickly by Lawyer or one of his headmen, who were beginning to prosper by selling services, livestock, and food supplies to newcomers. At the crossing of the Snake at present-day Lewiston, one headman named Reuben had gone into partnership with William Craig and was operating a ferry and warehouse for the incoming whites.

The mining area encompassed Nez Perce hunting, fishing, and gathering grounds but no permanent village sites, and Geary and Cain found Lawyer realistic about what was happening and not overly anxious to evict the miners. For "a big price," the head chief informed the agents, he would let the prospectors share the region of the mines. He settled for $50,000, and on April 10 he and forty-nine of his followers signed an ambiguously worded agreement with Geary and Cain, opening the reservation roughly north of the Clearwater River and the Lolo Trail to whites but reserving it also "for the exclusive use and benefit of the Indians." No whites were to be allowed elsewhere on the reservation. At the same time, Lawyer reminded the two agents that the Nez Perce had not yet received any of the funds or services that were already promised them by the 1855 treaty, and Geary promised to speed them up.

The new agreement was made quickly obsolete. As soon as the rush had begun, a new agency for the Nez Perce had been established on the site of Spalding's mission at the mouth of Lapwai Creek, but the subagent stationed there either could not, or would not, stem the frenetic mining expansion. On May 13 the stern-wheeler *Colonel Wright*, which had come up the Snake, unloaded passengers and goods on the south bank of the Clearwater at its junction with the Snake and a tent city, given the name Lewiston for Meriwether Lewis by a merchant named Vic Trevitt, sprang into existence. Lawyer protested the violation of the month-old agreement but acquiesced when he was given some "compensation" and a promise that no permanent structure would be built, an assurance that was soon forgotten.

That same month, prospectors, exploring far up the Clearwater and its south fork, invaded the countries of Lawyer's anti-white opponents deep within the reservation's southern reaches and made sensational new strikes north of the Salmon River. It started a series of new stampedes onto Indian lands, and such towns as Elk City and

Florence came into existence. As whites overran Nez Perce Country—building trails, wagon roads, ferries, overnight "hotels," saloons, stores, and log homes—anti-white headmen, including Eagle From the Light, White Bird, and Kulkulsní·nïn (Red Owl) protested and threatened to drive the miners away. But the situation had gotten beyond them. Members of their own bands, as well as Lawyer's followers, were being corrupted and changed swiftly by the inrush. In many of the villages and bands, Nez Perce culture and ways of life were altered almost overnight as some Indians participated in the excitement and boom economy. They supplied labor and food to the miners, visited their camps, helped them with pack trains, served as guides and messengers, ate the miners' food, drank their liquor, and wore their clothes. The whites paid them with gold dust, cash, trinkets, liquor, and favors, and though none grew wealthy by white standards, a number of Nez Perce, particularly some among Lawyer's followers who lived close to the main avenues of mining activity, benefited materially.

Yet all was not peaceful. Quarrels with the miners over livestock, land rights, springs, and other matters became frequent. Alcohol became a problem, and Indians, often made deliberately drunk, were cheated, robbed, and murdered. A succession of agents was powerless to protect the Nez Perce. "To attempt to restrain miners would be, to my mind, like attempting to restrain the whirlwind," one of them said. By June 1862 more than eighteen thousand whites were on the reservation, and friction had become so commonplace that some miners were calling on the government to move the Indians somewhere else. Blaming the situation on Lawyer, who was prospering and lording it over them, the anti-white chiefs met periodically in councils, and their threats to make war on the invaders heightened interracial tensions. Even Lawyer became unhappy. A payment for the 1855 treaty finally arrived in November 1862, but it was far less than promised. The goods were shoddy and were not enough to go around to his headmen, and most of the funds were diverted into the pockets of Cain and other whites. Though Lawyer objected, his complaints were lost amid a general corruption that then permeated the Indian Bureau.

In the meantime, having failed to back up the local agents and use troops to evict the miners, the political leaders in the Northwest had decided that an orderly government had to be established in the new mining districts and that, to do so, the title to the overrun lands had to be secured from the Indians. At their urging, Congress agreed in May 1862 to appropriate $50,000 to negotiate a new treaty with the Nez Perce to purchase more lands. In November, Lawyer and his headmen were informed bluntly that a council for such a purpose would be held at Lapwai the following spring. At the same time, troops were finally moved onto the reservation and stationed at a new military post, named Fort Lapwai, near the village of Craig's father-in-law, Thunder Eyes, in the Lapwai Valley. Rather than being used to force whites off the Indians' lands, the western volunteers were charged simply with policing against conflict, though in practice their presence worked to support the whites and instill further anxiety among the Indians.

The announcement of a new council shocked the Nez Perce. During the winter, concern and grim fears circulated among the bands of both factions as they remembered what had happened to the Wallawallas, Yakamas, and other tribes that had resisted eviction. The anti-white headmen berated Lawyer for the crisis, and he retorted that they had no respect for the laws of God or the American government. The breach widened.

When the council convened at Lapwai on May 25, 1863, none of the anti-white bands were present. The American commissioners included Calvin H. Hale, the superintendent of Indian Affairs in Washington Territory, and two Indian agents, Charles Hutchins and S. D. Howe. For interpreters they had selected Robert H. "Doc" Newell, a former mountain man and friend of Craig who had lived with the Nez Perce from time to time, and Henry Spalding, the former missionary who had been living in eastern Washington since 1859 and was now sixty years old. Spalding's wife, Eliza, had died in 1851, and

Spalding had married again. With the help of Timothy he had been agitating to be allowed to return to the Nez Perce. Lawyer and some of his headmen, however, felt that neither Newell nor Spalding had a good enough understanding of the Nez Perce language and, before the council started, prevailed on Hale to replace them with Marcus Whitman's nephew, Perrin, who had spent considerable time with the Nez Perce but who now lived on the lower Columbia River. To make "a good effect" on the Indians and give support to the commissioners, six companies of troops under Col. Justus Steinberger were also present, stationed at nearby Fort Lapwai.

While Perrin Whitman was sent for from his home, and in the absence of the anti-Lawyer bands, Spalding was allowed to interpret, and Hale opened the council by coming directly to the point. He told Lawyer and his headmen that he wanted the Nez Perce to compress themselves on a much smaller reservation, about one-tenth the size of the one they then possessed, based on the Clearwater, its south fork, and the Lapwai Valley, and situated tightly between the northern and southern mining districts. Those mining areas, together with all the rest of the Nez Perce reservation as constituted in 1855, would be purchased by the government and opened to whites. The bands would be paid for improvements on the lands. Moreover, the area within the new smaller reservation would be surveyed into eight-hectare (twenty-acre) lots, and one would be given to each family to farm "just as whites do."

Few of Lawyer's followers would be affected, for most of the their lands lay within the boundaries of the proposed new reservation. But the idea of bringing anti-Lawyer bands in among their own people stunned the assembled headmen. They would all be squeezed together, and there would be fights and endless turmoil. The headmen gave no answer, and the next day Hutchins repeated Hale's proposal, enumerating the payments the government would make. Responding at last, Yu·cınmé·lıxkın, the pro-Lawyer chief from Kamiah, and Lawyer questioned whether the commission actually spoke for the American government and pointed out that it was not adhering to the 1855 treaty and still owed the Nez Perce for the land the Indians had sold to the United States at that time. After several days of reviewing the Stevens treaty, during which Hale was forced to admit the government's delinquencies, Lawyer made a long and eloquent speech, relating the many times the Nez Perce had helped the Americans, asking for payments only for the ferries the whites were operating and the towns they had built on Nez Perce territory in violation of the 1855 treaty, and stating firmly that the Nez Perce could sell no more of their lands. Hale could not argue the head chief or his followers out of their position, and the council recessed for six days.

By the time it reconvened on June 3, a number of anti-Lawyer bands, including those of Joseph, Eagle From The Light, White Bird, and Red Owl, had arrived. Joined with them, also, was Thunder Eyes, who was against accepting the new reservation even though his Lapwai Valley lands would not be affected. He resented Lawyer, who had taken up residence on Thunder Eyes's land at the mouth of the Lapwai and was asserting a galling domination over the elderly chief. Perrin Whitman had also arrived, and he took over from Spalding as interpreter. After repeating his proposal for the newly arrived bands, Hale took a new tack, explaining that he wanted the bands to move together for their own safety. The government, he insisted speciously to the headmen, could not protect them from the aggressive miners if they remained spread widely apart. The chiefs listened patiently, then the leaders of both factions retired to a council of their own. When they returned, they announced that they would sell the land on which Lewiston was situated and the areas where gold had been found, but they could not further reduce the reservation.

Hale had reached an impasse with them, and after the council adjourned, he decided, as he wrote to Washington, to try "private conferences with the Chiefs, where, by direct questions and answers, there would be better opportunity of ascertaining their true feelings." In other words, he would pressure them, one by one. Beginning with "the leading chiefs of the friendly Indians," Lawyer and his individual headmen, he worked on them that night in private sessions. With the help of Spalding and Whitman, he hammered at them persuasively, exploiting their jealousies and divisions and offering gifts and favors until, individually, they agreed to sign the treaty. His principal argument was that none of them would lose anything, for all their villages, save those of Timothy and Jason, lay within the new reservation. Since Timothy and Jason were considered to be almost white men, Hale agreed that they both could stay where they were on their farms at Alpowa, outside the reservation, and he promised them money with which to build themselves new homes.

His success with the Lawyer faction almost came apart the next day. The anti-Lawyer headmen learned what was happening, and during the day Hale found some backsliding among those who had given him their word the night before. In renewed private talks, he managed to regain their acceptance of the treaty, but by then, the anti-Lawyer headmen deeply resented Hale's tactics. That night, the leaders of both factions held a council. A soldier on the grounds overheard some of the deliberations and reported that "the debate ran with dignified firmness and warmth until next morning," when Thunder Eyes, speaking for the anti-Lawyer chiefs, "with a warm, and in an emotional manner, declared the Nez Perce nation *dissolved;* whereupon the Big Thunder [Thunder Eyes] men shook hands with the Lawyer men, telling them with a kind but firm demeanor that they would be friends, but a distinct people."

It was a further, and definitive, confirmation of the splitting of the Nez Perce into two factions, which thereafter became known as "the treaty group" and "the non-treaty group." The next morning, Joseph and White Bird, neither of whom had said anything during the two sessions of the council they had attended, left Lapwai with their people and went home. Before his departure, Joseph tore up his copies of the Stevens treaty of 1855 and the Gospel of Matthew, which Spalding had printed at Lapwai years before and given to him when he had first baptized him, and which Joseph had carried with him ever since. They were more than symbolic gestures. Joseph had lost all faith in the word of the Americans, and their religion now seemed to him to have been used hypocritically as a tool to rob him of his country. Neither he nor White Bird had any intention of selling their lands, which lay outside the new reservation's boundaries, and it would never have occurred to them that anyone who remained behind at Lapwai, including Lawyer, would have asserted the right to speak for them or assumed an illegal authority to sign away their lands in their absence. Moreover, there were other anti-Lawyer bands whose lands the commissioners wanted but who had not come to the council and may not even have known about the meeting. None of them, either, would have believed that someone else could give away their country.

That, however, is just what happened. After Joseph and White Bird left, the commissioners went to work on Thunder Eyes, Eagle From The Light, and the few other remaining anti-Lawyer headmen, charging them with "disloyalty" and threatening them with severe punishment and humiliation if they refused to sign the treaty. The brow-beating was unconscionable, but finally worked. Aided by Newell, the commissioners convinced the holdouts that their own lands lay within the new reservation and they would lose nothing. One after the other, they assented to the treaty, though to demonstrate their independence of Lawyer, they won the right not to have to put their marks on the document. On June 9, Lawyer and fifty-one members of his faction signed the treaty. Since there had been fifty-three headmen of both factions at the night session when the tribe had divided, and none of the anti-Lawyer group signed, it was evident that Lawyer had rounded up a number of his lesser men to sign.

Hale immediately informed the Commissioner of Indian Affairs in Washington how cheaply he had accomplished his mission: "Nearly six million acres . . . obtained at a cost not exceeding eight cents per acre," he wrote proudly. Later surveyors claimed that he had gotten 2,804,786 hectares (6,932,270 acres) from the Nez Perce in Idaho, Oregon, and Washington and left the Nez Perce with 317,611 hectares (784,999 acres), slightly more than 25 percent of the 1855 reservation. But he had raised a large question that would spell trouble in future years—and still causes bitter conflict. He had conferred on Lawyer the right and obligation to speak for all the bands and to sign away all the lands of Joseph, White Bird, and every other Nez Perce, save Timothy and Jason, who lived outside the new reservation.

Lawyer had neither objected to that act nor explained that he did not possess the right to do what he had done. On the contrary, there is evidence that Lawyer had come to the conclusion that he wanted the non-Christians on the reservation, where he and the agent—and the troops, if necessary—could control them. Again and again he had complained about the bad influences that the young men of the anti-Lawyer bands had on his own people. In their own countries, they lived beyond the reach of the authority of the laws and the Americans. If they were forced onto the reservation, they could be punished and taught the right ways to behave. With the help of the agent, he also could more easily bring their headmen and chiefs under his own domination.

The treaty he signed gave the bands one year after its ratification to move onto the reservation. Tillable lands on the reservation would be allotted, and the tribe would hold the rest of the land in common. The government would only have to pay the tribe $265,000 for all the ceded land, and more than half of it would be appropriated in four installments to fund the moving of the off-reservation bands and to pay for the preparation of the allotments—a diversion of payments, in part, from the bands that were supposed to give up lands to those that were not. In effect, some of the money was spent for bands that still retained their lands. In addition, funds were promised for agricultural equipment, a sawmill, a schoolhouse, headmen's houses, a blacksmith shop, salaries, and the payment for the horses used in the wars of the 1850s—a reiteration of the same promises, still unkept, that had been made by the Stevens treaty, though this time most of the funds would go directly to the Lawyer faction. Finally, the Nez Perce signatories had agreed that the whites could build roads, ferries, and other public improvements, as well as inns for the miners, anywhere on the shrunken reservation.

The new treaty was fraudulent on the part of both Lawyer and the commissioners. The latter had practiced coercion, bribery, and deceit, and though Lawyer later protested lamely that he had not meant to sign in behalf of the absent bands, his conduct belied that assertion. Word that he had signed for the entire tribe was conveyed to Washington without qualification, and Lawyer never straightened out the record. In actuality, Joseph and the other nonsignatory bands outside the new boundary line had their lands sold out from under them by Lawyer, who was promised a disproportionate share of the treaty's meager beneficence.

The announcement of the new agreement made the situation more chaotic than before. Despite Hale's promises, preoccupation with the Civil War and other matters held up the Senate's ratification of the treaty, and it was not until April 20, 1867, four years after the Lapwai council, that President Andrew Johnson signed the document. In the meantime, numerous whites, unwilling to wait for ratification, invaded many parts of the country that were going to be ceded, squatting among the non-treaties and pressing in around the borders of what would become the new reservation. Friction and conflicts increased, as did the cheating and killing of Indians. Whites seized the property of both the treaties and non-treaties, appropriated their grazing lands, timber, and sources of water, stole their livestock, and claimed their orchards, gardens, village sites, and fishing stations. In areas that settlers found particularly attractive, like the fertile Camas Prairie and grassy benches of the Snake and Salmon river valleys, the Indians' possession of the land was seriously contested by white homeseekers, who did not wait for the formalities of a government survey that would precede an official opening of the country to settlement. They put up houses and fences and warned the Nez Perce to stay away. In other, more remote regions, like Joseph's Wallowa Valley, the Nez Perce had a longer period of grace.

Since the treaty had not been ratified, the anti-treaty bands who lived off the reservation were not forced to move onto it. Save for the social visiting and communal gatherings at root grounds and fishing sites, the breach between them and the Lawyer bands was almost complete, ameliorated only by continued contacts between relatives and friends. In large measure, the non-treaties went their own way, ignoring Lawyer and his headmen, trying to cope with the aggressive expansion of the whites, and continuing to follow many of their old ways. Some of them built up large herds of cattle, but they hunted

and fished regularly and still crossed the mountains to hunt buffalo
and visit friends among the plains tribes.

Lawyer had many problems of his own. Not only was he not receiving payments for the huge 1863 land cession, but the government
was again derelict in observing promises of the 1855 treaty. When
driblets did arrive, they were embezzled by a series of corrupt agents.
Even Caleb Lyon, the Federally-appointed governor of Idaho, which
had become a territory in 1863, managed to abscond with $46,418.40
of the Nez Perce' money. Moreover, Lawyer's headmen seethed over
the way their people were mistreated and their property and resources
stolen. They had numerous complaints for the head chief, ranging
from the presence on the reservation of whisky sellers to whites who
cut down Indian-owned trees without paying. At the same time, they
reminded Lawyer that the Nez Perce could expect no protection from
the Americans' laws or courts.

Though Lawyer made many special appeals to officials who visited the reservation, he got no satisfaction. Soon after the ratification
of the 1863 treaty, he addressed a letter to President Johnson asking if
he could travel to Washington to confer about the wrongs his people
were suffering. Since it happened that the government then wished to
amend the recently approved 1863 treaty to acquire more reservation
land for a permanent military post at Fort Lapwai, the Commissioner
of Indian Affairs thought it was a good idea to take the head chief to
the East, where he could see how strong the United States was and
perhaps prove more amenable to making another land sale. In March
1868, accompanied by agent James O'Neill and interpreters Robert
Newell and Perrin Whitman, Lawyer, Timothy, Jason, and Yu·cınmé·
lıxkın left Lapwai and journeyed to the national capital by way of
Portland, San Francisco, Panama, and New York. In May, Yu·cınmé·
lıxkın died of typhoid and was buried in Washington. But the other
three Nez Perce signed a new agreement on August 13, ceding land
for the military post and receiving assurances of protection of their
timber, of additional 8–hectare (20–acre) lots off the reservation if
there was not enough room for everyone once the non-treaty bands
moved on the reserve, and of making good Nez Perce Indian school

funds that had been stolen by white officials. No non-treaty band leader was among the Indian delegation, or signed the new agreement. Once again, Lawyer and his followers had assumed to speak for every band. Newell, whom the Lawyer faction trusted, was appointed the tribe's new agent, and the party left Washington on August 22, reaching home via railroad and stage on September 22. As the Indian Commissioner had surmised, the might and power of the American nation and the size of its eastern cities had not been lost on the three Nez Perce. More than ever, they were proud to be friends of so strong a country.

The ratification of the treaty and its amendments did little to ease conditions. The long-delayed government payments, goods, and services began finally to reach Lawyer and his headmen, but conflicts with the whites continued, and the treaty bands remained anxious about their future, fearful of the threatened allotment of the reservation, their forced dispersal onto small individual lots, and the opening of the rest of their country to whites. A lack of funds kept postponing the surveying of the reservation into lots, but even that distressed Lawyer. Until the lots were marked off, the non-treaties could stay off the reservation, where they were free to make trouble, as he saw it, and influence the treaty Indians. He repeatedly complained about the "wild" and "heathen" Nez Perce, and the agents kept promising him that they would soon be forced onto the reservation.

In 1869–70, the pressure of reformers and religious leaders in the East led President Ulysses S. Grant to adopt a new "peace" policy in dealing with tribes. Under it, the government, violating the doctrine of separation of church and state, parceled out the reservations to different religious denominations, delegating to them the right to nominate the agents and administer tribal affairs. It was hoped that the churches would end the corruption and injustices that caused Indian hostility, as well as hasten the conversion of Indians to Christianized farmers and their assimilation into white society.

The decision soon affected the Nez Perce, whose administration was awarded to the Presbyterians. The man they chose to be agent, John B. Monteith, a strong-willed son of a Presbyterian minister, arrived on the reservation in February 1871, determined to continue and strengthen the Presbyterian influence. Once again, Henry Spalding, the pioneer Presbyterian missionary, would play a role. After the treaty of 1863, Hale had appointed Spalding government school-teacher at the Lapwai agency. But Spalding, who had grown increasingly cantankerous and dictatorial, fought with the agent and others, was grossly inadequate as a secular teacher, and was dismissed by the agent in 1865. Soon afterward, Catholic priests had had success in converting some of the treaty Nez Perce, but when they wanted to found a mission on the reservation, they were opposed by Lawyer and were forced to settle in Lewiston and administer principally to whites. Still, they maintained influence among a few bands.

In 1870 George Waters, a young Yakama Methodist preacher, and three of his followers conducted a series of emotional revival meetings that inspired an interest in Christianity among many treaty Indians. When Monteith arrived, he ordered the Yakama Methodists to leave, but Father Joseph M. Cataldo, a Jesuit priest who came down from his church among the Coeur d'Alene Indians, and Henry Spalding, assisted by Henry T. Cowley, a young, newly arrived Presbyterian missionary, heightened the Christian fervor that the Yakamas had awakened. Competing fiercely against each other, both Spalding and Cataldo made many converts among the Nez Perce treaty element. Until 1873, however, Monteith refused to let the Catholics build a mission. Finally, the government overruled him, and in 1874 Father Cataldo opened St. Joseph's Mission about 6 kilometers (4 miles) south of present-day Jacques, Idaho, in the Sweetwater Valley above Lapwai. Built on the land of a headman who had converted his entire Presbyterian following to Catholicism, it was referred to as the Slick-poo Mission in his honor.

At the same time, Cowley established a mission home and school at Kamiah, where in 1871 a number of Presbyterian Nez Perce were organized into the First Presbyterian Church of Kamiah. Cowley quarreled with Monteith and in early 1873 was replaced as teacher and missionary by Spalding. The church structure, which is today the oldest continually used Presbyterian church in Idaho, was completed the next year. That same year, after baptizing more than six hundred Nez Perce, Spalding became ill, returned to Lapwai, and died there on August 3, 1874, at the age of seventy-one. He was buried close to the location of his early mission at present-day Spalding, the site of the Nez Perce National Historical Park headquarters.

During the same period, Lawyer's role as head chief ended. He was growing old, and many of his followers were turning away from him. In the fall of 1871, a council of the treaty leaders finally deposed him but was unable to agree on a successor. The next year, over Lawyer's objection, it managed to elect a new head chief, Jacob, who was not a Christian. Lawyer moved back to Kamiah, but in 1874 the council deposed Jacob, and Lawyer, at Monteith's request, unofficially reassumed the position of head chief until 1875, when the council chose Reuben, a Christian. Reuben was also the brother-in-law of Old Joseph's son, the new Chief Joseph, who had become leader of the non-treaty Wallowa band, but the two men did not agree on their relations with whites or the American government. Lawyer finally died at Kamiah on January 3, 1876, at about age eighty and was buried in the cemetery of the Presbyterian church, of which he was an elder. His death was mourned by the treaty faction and by whites, who eulogized him as a loyal friend. Though the results of that friendship and the role he played in critical periods of Nez Perce history have made him a controversial figure, he continues to loom large as a patriot who felt that the only way to save his people was to follow the road of the whites as a firm friend of the American government. A true perspective on him, however, is far from settled; to those who were hurt by him or lost their lands as a result of his actions, he is still considered a man who betrayed the Nez Perce.

The sudden surge of Christianity on the reservation created a quarrelsome division between Presbyterians and Catholics among the reservation Nez Perce and hardened the anti-Christian feelings of the non-treaties. At one point, the new Chief Joseph rebuffed a suggestion that a white man's school be provided for his people in the Wallowa Valley. He did not want schools, he said, because they taught the Nez Perce to want churches, and he did not want churches because "they will teach us to quarrel about God, as the Catholics and Protestants do on the Nez Perce reservation, and at other places. We do not want to learn that. We may quarrel with men sometimes about things on this earth, but we never quarrel about God. We do not want to learn that."

On the reservation, the new interest in Christianity resulted undoubtedly from the tensions and anxieties through which the people had been living. The government-supported headmen took the lead in accepting Christianity, bringing their entire villages and bands along with them in mass conversions that allowed them to retain their leadership positions, though in new roles of pastors, preachers, and elders. The acceptance of Christianity, moreover, gave them a sense of increased security. Because the agent was a Presbyterian and the reservation was under the Presbyterians' control, there seemed obvious advantages, politically and economically, in becoming a Presbyterian.

The spread of Christianity brought other changes. Ancient village sites were abandoned as bands clustered in new family dwellings—sometimes log huts—around the churches. In these new church-village centers, the former headmen vied for prestigious positions as church leaders. The new factionalism and antagonisms that broke out between the Catholics and Protestants were exacerbated by the Catholics' awareness of the Protestants' superior power. And, finally, the dogma and regulations of the churches hastened acculturation. Old habits and ways, beliefs, manners of dress, and cultural traits were ridiculed and proscribed as pagan, heathenish, and backward. Even the use of horses and the acceptance of chiefs were eventually frowned upon or condemned.

All this was in marked contrast to the state of the non-treaties, whom the Christian factions referred to as "heathens." The anxieties of the non-treaties, and some other Plateau tribes, had also given rise to various new nativistic cults, most of them stemming again from the earlier Prophet cults. Whites became particularly aware of one of them, which they called the Dreamer religion and which had been spread by a Wanapum Indian shaman named Smohalla, who lived at Priest Rapids on the Columbia. Like the prophets of most cults, Smohalla claimed he had died, had received certain instructions in the afterworld, and had then returned to life to communicate those instructions to the Indians. By abandoning the customs and clothing of the white man and returning to the ways of their ancestors, by following pure and sacred rules of behavior, and by participating in special dances and using prescribed symbolic objects in their rituals, the Indians, he asserted, would be rewarded with a new day of peace when the white man and his works would disappear from their lands.

By the 1870s, male and female shamans were preaching somewhat similar messages to many of the non-treaty bands, including Joseph's. The cults and the degree of their acceptance varied from tribe to tribe and, among the non-treaty Nez Perce, from band to band, but the whites tended to see them all as part of a single conspiracy, preached by Smohalla, with the aim of uniting all of the Northwest Indians in an uprising against the whites. By the early 1870s, many American political and military leaders thought the principal agents of such an uprising would be the non-treaty Nez Perce, who were the most powerful Indians still living off reservations. And their attention suddenly focused on Joseph's band in the Wallowa Valley in northeastern Oregon, where conflict with whites, seemingly more serious than in Idaho, had at last erupted.

Actually, the tragic drama of what was occurring in the Wallowa Valley was already bedeviling agent Monteith, making scare headlines in papers across the Northwest and perplexing officials in Washington DC, and Portland. Old Joseph, one of Spalding's first two converts, but again a "heathen" in the eyes of the Christian reservation Nez Perce, died in August 1871 insisting that he had never sold his homeland. "Always remember that your father never sold his country," he told his son and successor, the thirty-one-year-old Hinmató· wyalahtq̓ıt (Thunder Traveling to Loftier Mountain Heights), whom the whites would soon know as Young Joseph or Chief Joseph. "You must stop your ears whenever you are asked to sign a treaty selling your home. A few years more, and white men will be all around you.

His eloquent pleas for justice and equality made Joseph one of the most well-known Indian leaders in North America. Courtesy National Anthropological Archives, Smithsonian Institution (neg. no. 2907).

They have their eyes on this land. My son, never forget my dying words. This country holds your father's body. Never sell the bones of your father and your mother."

Even as Old Joseph was buried, however, the first white settlers were finding a route into the valley from Oregon's Grande Ronde country. More of them came the next year, and the next, building homes, seizing pasturage for their stock, and telling the youthful Joseph, his younger brother ʔalokat, who was the hunting and war leader of the young men, and the other members of the band that the government had purchased the area from the tribe in 1863 and the Indians would have to leave. The leaders of the band, which numbered approximately 250 people, argued in a series of councils with the settlers that they had never sold the land. Monteith was summoned from Lapwai, 160 kilometers (100 miles) away, to straighten out the facts and was nonplussed when he realized what had actually happened at the 1863 council. The commissioners had maintained, and the government in Washington had believed, that Lawyer had had the right to sign for every band, selling the lands of bands whose leaders had not signed the treaty. But did Lawyer really have the right to do so?

Seriously questioning whether he could legally oust either the Indians or the settlers from the Wallowa, but deploring the fact that the valley had ever been opened to whites, Monteith wrote to the Commissioner of Indian Affairs, telling him of the confusion and stating that "if there is any way by which the Wallowa Valley could be kept for the Indians, I would recommend that it be done." His report persuaded the Department of the Interior that the government's title to Joseph's land was, at best, questionable and led to an administration decision on June 16, 1873, to divide the area into two sections, one for the white settlers and the other as a permanent reservation for Joseph's band. A provision was also made to purchase the improvements of any settler who had to move.

The proposal was seen as an abject surrender to potentially hostile Indians and raised a storm of protest among the whites in the valley, as well as in newspapers throughout the Northwest. Joseph was an unusual man. Born in 1840 in a cave near the mouth of present-day Joseph Creek in the Wallowa country, he was tall, heavily built, and had handsome, noble features and an imposing presence. He had inherited his father's tolerance, compassion, and gentle manner and was a civil, rather than a hunting or military, chief. He carried himself with dignity, could speak with eloquence and logic, and was already known among the non-treaties as a man of wisdom and peace. But white public opinion throughout the Northwest suddenly had a new Indian villain. As a non-treaty who refused to go on the reservation, he was considered a dangerous and scheming "hostile" and a follower of the much-feared Smohalla, who at any moment might start a general uprising.

As a result of the settlers' protest and pressure from Oregon's political leaders, the Grant Administration on June 10, 1875, did an about-face and rescinded the 1873 order that divided the Wallowa, giving Monteith the duty of informing Joseph that his people, along with all the other off-reservation, non-treaty bands, would have to go onto the reservation even though it had still not been surveyed into allotments. Refusing to do so, Joseph met again and again with the Wallowa settlers, trying to persuade them that his people had never sold their homeland, but to no avail. At times, he also met with the headmen and chiefs of the other non-treaty bands, including Eagle From The Light and Looking Glass, whose lands were on the reservation, and such off-reservation leaders as White Bird from the Salmon River country and Tuhuhulcú·t, a tall, powerful shaman who headed a band in the mountainous country between the Snake and Salmon rivers east of the Wallowa. A few headmen and their war chiefs were all for joining other tribes in armed resistance against the whites, but the majority, including Joseph, refused to agree to war even though they would not go onto the reservation. Clinging to the hope that he could settle his own problem peaceably and arguing persistently that the Americans would destroy any band that took up arms, Joseph displeased some of the other off-reservation leaders. They suspected that he, like Lawyer, might become too defeatist and pro-white to be a reliable ally.

Meanwhile, the Wallowa Valley crisis mounted. The scares of an Indian war increased among the settlers, and several times they panicked and sent for troops, who hastened into the valley, found the scares unwarranted, and left after chiding the settlers. On some occasions, the military leaders who studied the conflict filed reports that were more sympathetic to the Indians than the settlers. In August 1875, Capt. Stephen C. Whipple, who was ordered to the valley by Gen. Oliver O. Howard, the new commander of the Department of the Columbia at Fort Vancouver, satisfied himself that Joseph was telling the truth when he said that his people had never sold their land. When Whipple wrote his report, Howard sent it on to the War Department with comments of his own: "I think it a great mistake to take from Joseph and his band of Nez Perce Indians that valley . . . possibly Congress can be induced to let these really peaceable Indians have this poor valley for their own." Soon afterward, Howard sent his assistant adjutant general, Maj. Henry Clay Wood, to the valley to make a legal study of the causes of the unrest. After lengthy research, Wood reported, "In my opinion . . . the non-treaty Nez Perce cannot in law be regarded as bound by the treaty of 1863; and in so far as it attempts to deprive them of a right to occupancy of any land its provisions are null and void. The extinguishment of their title of occupancy contemplated by this treaty is imperfect and incomplete."

The danger of a new Indian war preyed on Howard's mind. A deeply religious and moralistic man, he was particularly moved by a letter from the Rev. A. L. Lindsley, a prominent Presbyterian minister in Portland who kept in touch with Monteith and was familiar with the Wallowa situation. The Joseph band's "title has never been rightfully extinguished," Lindsley wrote. "In fact, the fair construction of treaty stipulations confirms the Indian title. . . . The treaty of 1863 was not adopted by the Nez Perce tribe, but by a part only. . . . The Government is bound by its own engagement to fulfill the original Treaty [of 1855], until it can procure an honorable discharge from its obligations." Lindsley, who like Monteith wanted the non-treaties to go onto the reservation under Presbyterian care, concluded by proposing that the government appoint a new commission to buy the

Wallowa Valley from the Indians, which would make everything just and honorable.

The proposal appealed to Howard, particularly when the crisis was heightened in June 1876 by the murder of one of Joseph's close friends, Wilhautyah (Wind Blowing), by two Wallowa settlers, who assumed erroneously that he had stolen some of their horses. When the horses turned up soon afterward, the settlers again panicked. Moving quickly to avert a showdown, Howard sent word to Joseph to meet with Wood and other military officers at Lapwai. Joseph, ʔalokat, and some forty members of the Wallowa band journeyed angrily to the post, but they agreed to let the Americans bring the murderers to justice. At the same time, Wood and the other officers showed their sympathy and respect for the statesmanlike Joseph, who seemed satisfied by their assurances and pleased that Howard was recommending to Washington that the President appoint a commission to settle all difficulties.

Two months passed, however, before the murderers of Wilhautyah were forced to give themselves up to a court in the Grande Ronde, and then one of them was released without a trial and the other was exonerated. The long delay and the freeing of the two men, coupled with boastful threats made by irresponsible settlers to scalp Joseph and drive his people out of the valley, brought the Indians and the whites to the brink of bloodshed several times. Joseph and ʔalokat' found it increasingly difficult to restrain their young men, and once more Howard had to send troops into the valley. Finally, in September, Howard traveled to Washington to press for the creation of a commission, and in October the Secretary of the Interior acceded, setting up a five-member group, including Howard and Wood, to buy Joseph's land as a prelude to moving all the off-reservation bands onto the reservation.

The commission met at Lapwai on November 13, 1876, with Joseph, ʔalokat, some sixty members of the Wallowa band, and a few members of the other non-treaty bands. The meeting was doomed to failure, for Joseph frustrated and angered Howard and the rest of the commissioners, save Wood, by reiterating his claim of ownership of the Wallowa and his refusal to sell it. In later years, he stated what he tried to explain to the commissioners: "Suppose a white man should come to me and say, 'Joseph, I like your horses, and I want to buy them.' I say to him, 'No, my horses suit me, I will not sell them.' Then he goes to my neighbor, and says to him: 'Joseph has some good horses. I want to buy them, but he refuses to sell.' My neighbor answers, 'Pay me the money, and I will sell you Joseph's horses.' The white man returns to me and says, 'Joseph, I have bought your horses, and you must let me have them.' If we sold our lands to the Government, this is the way they were bought."

The argument of ownership seemed irrelevant to the commissioners, but when Joseph made it equally clear that his people would never sell their homeland, the council ended. The exasperated commissioners then recommended to the Department of the Interior that Joseph's people and the other off-reservation bands be directed to move onto the reservation "within a reasonable time," after which force should be used to move them. The commissioners, who had listened to Monteith, various missionaries, and some of the Christian Nez Perce, also characterized the non-treaty bands as being under the influence of Smohalla's Dreamer "sorcerers," and they recommended that the Dreamer religious leaders be suppressed or exiled to the Indian Territory in present-day Oklahoma.

With the Interior Department's concurrence, Monteith interpreted the "reasonable time" as April 1, 1877, and sent four treaty Nez Perce, including the head chief, Reuben, who was Joseph's brother-in-law, Reuben's son James, Joseph's father-in-law, and Captain John, to tell Joseph to come onto the reservation by that date or Howard would use troops to force him to move. Thinking that there must be some mistake, since Howard and his officers had several times made known their understanding of the Indians' right to the Wallowa country, Joseph made a number of attempts to meet Howard again and see if he really meant to use the army against his people. Mindful of the Little Bighorn disaster to Custer's troops the previous year, when the army had tried to rush the Sioux onto reservations, Howard was willing to give the Nez Perce plenty of time, and he agreed to meet with the off-reservation bands once more at Fort Lapwai on May 3, well after Monteith's deadline.

It was a last and fateful gathering. The non-treaty chiefs met first and selected Tuhuhulcú·t, an uncompromising and able orator, to be their spokesman. Then, painted, dressed in their finery, and singing proudly, the bands rode, one by one, to Fort Lapwai, where crowds of treaty Nez Perce and whites watched their arrival with concern and awe. If the non-treaties thought that Monteith had been wrong and that troops would not be used against them, Howard soon disabused them of the belief. Telling them sternly that they would now have to go on the reservation or he would drive them on, he got into an angry altercation with Tuhuhulcú·t, treating him insultingly, and finally seized him and propelled him rudely into the post guardhouse. The display of intemperance and force against their spokesman stunned and angered the chiefs and their people. Howard had turned enemy and had "showed them the rifle." As they sat in silence, they realized that it was now time to give up their lands, or fight.

Concern for the safety of their women, children, and old people, many of whom were with them, finally moved the chiefs to accept the inevitable. They agreed reluctantly to move peaceably. Then they rode over the reservation for several days, selecting sites on which their bands would settle. Howard gave them only thirty days to move even though the Snake, the Salmon, and other rivers would be in full spring floodtide and the crossings of people and their possessions and livestock would be perilous. He then released Tuhuhulcú·t. The bands, torn with sadness and anger, rode home to pack up, gather their stock, and leave the lands of their forefathers.

Many of the young men wanted to fight, but councils of the chiefs and elders convinced them that resistance would be hopeless. In the Salmon River country, where the miners and settlers had long been murdering, cheating, and mistreating members of White Bird's band, the departing Indians smoldered with hatred for many of the whites.

For two days, Joseph's people struggled across the raging torrent of the Snake River, losing many of their possessions and horses and cattle. Then they crossed the Salmon, headed up Rocky Canyon to

Tıpaʔx̣líwam (Split Rocks), the ancient counciling site at the camas meadows beside Tolo Lake about 10 kilometers (6 miles) west of present-day Grangeville, Idaho. There, on June 2, twelve days before they had to be on the reservation, most of the non-treaty bands—some six hundred people, two-thirds of them women, children, and old men—rendezvoused.

As the days passed, their anger rose. On June 12, with only two days left, a number of young men conducted a te·lıklí·kse parade ceremony, riding around the camp, showing off their battle trophies and proudly recounting their war deeds. One, Wá·laytıc, was taunted by an elderly warrior for riding in the parade when he had not avenged the murder of his father by a white man in the Salmon River country. That night, the youth brooded over the challenge and at dawn enlisted two other young men, including his cousin, Sá·psus ʔılp̓ílp. Riding back to the Salmon River area, they hunted in vain for the slayer of Wá·laytıc's father, then killed four white men and wounded another, all known for their mistreatment of Indians.

Their return to Tıpaʔx̣líwam and announcement of what they had done threw the camp into excitement. Joseph and ʔalokat were not there, having recrossed the Salmon to butcher some cattle that they had left behind. Among all the bands, however, there was hasty councils. The three youths were members of White Bird's band, and already a larger group of warriors, mostly from the same band, was forming to go back to the Salmon River and kill more whites who had injured their people. As the new party of seventeen members, including Cú·hım maqsmáqs (Yellow Bull), a noted warrior, rode off, the non-treaties began to collect their goods and hurry to a safer location. Howard would soon hear about the killings. The war that the chiefs had tried to avoid had begun.

Chapter Seven
War Comes to the Non-Treaties

On June 14–15, the second group of raiding Nez Perce continued the work of the first, killing or wounding more than a dozen other whites along the Salmon River with whom they had scores to settle. Word of their angry retribution sped through the countryside, in one case being carried to the miners at Florence by an alarmed Nez Perce woman named Tolo, who feared the consequences of the warriors' actions. Sure that the long-expected uprising by the non-treaties was underway, the whites barricaded themselves in an improvised stockade at Slate Creek on the Salmon or fled to Mount Idaho, the nearest large settlement on the Camas Prairie, and sent messengers to Fort Lapwai for help.

Joseph and ʔalokat, meanwhile, had returned to Tıpaʔx̣líwam to learn with horror what had happened and to see all the people, save their own, dispersing for safety. Christian and reservation Nez Perce, who had been visiting friends and relatives among the non-treaties, hastened back to the reservation to proclaim their disapproval of the violence. Some members of the band of Looking Glass, known to the Nez Perce as ʔelelímyeteʔqenıń, who had been outspokenly against opposing Howard, hurried to join their chief at a root-gathering camp at Clear Creek on the Middle Fork of the Clearwater, at the southeastern extremity of the reservation near present-day Kooskia, where they hoped to avoid the trouble that was sure to come. The rest, including the bands of White Bird and Tuhuhulcú·t, moved across the Camas Prairie to a large cavern named Sapáʔca·s (Drive-In) on Cottonwood Creek above its junction with the Clearwater's South

Fork, where Nez Perce warriors had once trapped and annihilated some raiding Bannocks.

Only the Wallowa band remained at Tıpa'x̱lı́wam. For a while, Joseph, ʔalokat, and others thought that if they could meet with Howard they could convince the general not to punish all the people for the hot-headed actions of a few young men—including one of their own, Lahpeealoot (Geese Three Times Lighting on Water). That night, however, shots fired at their tipis convinced them that the whites were too inflamed to listen to them, and in the morning they decided, for the safety of their women, children, and old men, to join the other non-treaties. Enduring injustice, persecution, and provocations, Joseph and ʔalokat had done all they could to stay at peace. Perhaps if Howard pursued them, the non-treaties would still have a chance to parley with him before he attacked them. Meanwhile, Joseph and his people set off for Cottonwood Creek, determined to stay with the other non-treaty bands in their hour of peril. Soon after they reached Sapáʔca·s, all the bands headed for greater security to Lamáta, White Bird's campsite near the junction of White Bird Creek and the Salmon River, close to the present-day town of White Bird. The site was protected by a series of ridges and hills across the long, open, descending plains of White Bird Canyon, and was backed by the Salmon, across which the bands could withdraw if necessary.

Hope of an understanding with Howard was unrealistic. By the time the bands reached White Bird, terror had spread across the Camas Prairie. War parties of Nez Perce, guarding the movements of the bands, had attacked white teamsters, messengers, and fleeing families on the roads between Lewiston, Cottonwood, Grangeville, and Mount Idaho. Some warriors had become drunk on liquor they had seized in their raids and had committed atrocities that had raised the whites' anti-Indian feelings to a fevered pitch. A group of volunteers, led by Arthur "Ad" Chapman, a Salmon River settler married to a Umatilla Indian, had been organized at Mount Idaho, and in the frenzied skirmishing on the Prairie, a number of whites and one Indian had been killed.

General Howard had returned to Fort Lapwai on June 14 from the lower Columbia and was certain that within a day or so the non-treaties would arrive peaceably on the reservation. Word of the depredations came as a shock, not only to him, but to the whites around Lewiston and the various elements of the reservation Nez Perce, many of whom crowded into the agency, fearing that the non-treaties were about to attack the reservation. Howard was willing to accept their protestations that the non-treaties were "bad Indians" and "trouble-makers," but he knew that a successful uprising could be contagious. Without direct contact with, or knowledge of, what was occurring among the non-treaties, he was quick to ascribe the outburst to deliberate treachery by his principal, and best-known, opponent, Joseph, and was determined to nip the trouble before it spread to all disaffected Indians throughout the Northwest.

Moving quickly on the evening of June 15, he dispatched Capt. David Perry from Fort Lapwai with two troops of the 1st U.S. Cavalry, F and H companies, totaling 103 enlisted men, to put an end to the Indian killings and provide safety for the settlers. With Perry went a mule train, an interpreter, and eleven unarmed reservation Nez Perce, who were to act as intermediaries to help convince the non-treaties to stop fighting. At the same time, to assemble a force large enough to crush the non-treaty Nez Perce and thwart a serious uprising, he called in a cavalry unit that he had previously stationed in the Wallowa and sent to Walla Walla and Portland for reinforcements. Howard also wired Gen. Irvin McDowell, commander of the Division of the Pacific in San Francisco, an account of the murders and ended, "Think we will make short work of it."

Perry hurried his column through the night and the next day to Grangeville on the Camas Prairie and rested there a few hours. Then, goaded by frightened settlers, who also blamed Chief Joseph for directing the uprising, Perry started out in search of the non-treaties, who he was told were now at White Bird and should be attacked and defeated before they could escape into the mountains on the opposite side of the Salmon River. Accompanied by Chapman and ten citizen volunteers, the weary troops reached the summit of White Bird Hill about midnight and stopped once more, intending to attack down the slope at dawn. As the troopers settled down in silence, they heard the howl of a coyote, "enough to make one's hair stand straight up," said one of Perry's men. The troopers guessed rightly that it was a signal cry from a Nez Perce lookout who had seen them.

The Nez Perce camp lay far down the rolling slope, hidden behind ridges and buttes. Soon after the coyote signal sounded, a Nez Perce sentinel raced into camp with word that the soldiers were coming. The chiefs realized that the future of their people was at stake and apparently all agreed with Joseph that an attempt should be made to parley peaceably with the troops. Though some Nez Perce later denied it, others, including the warrior Yellow Wolf, maintained that six men were detailed to carry forward a white flag of truce and to try to arrange a peaceful talk with the soldiers when they appeared in the morning. If that failed, then the Indians would stand and defend their people.

The total manpower of the combined bands was about 135, but many warriors were lying helplessly drunk from whisky they had seized and would still not be able to fight at dawn. Others had no weapons. Altogether, not more than sixty or seventy Indians possessed arms, mostly bows and arrows and antiquated shotguns and muzzle-loading fur-trade muskets. Ammunition was scarce, and since no bullet could be wasted, it was agreed that the veteran fighters and best marksmen would use the guns, while the boys and young men would take care of the noncombatants and the large herds of horses and cattle they had brought with them from their homes. During the battle, the war leaders would hide their followers on both flanks of the advancing troops and direct their actions. No single chief was to direct all the fighting.

At 4 a.m. on June 17, Perry's command commenced its long descent of the slope, with Lt. Edward Theller leading an advance guard of eight cavalrymen, trumpeter John Jones, several treaty Nez Perce, and volunteer Arthur Chapman. According to Yellow Wolf and others, the Nez Perce truce team, backed by other warriors, had ridden out to meet them and were eventually seen by Theller's group when it topped a ridge about two-thirds down the slope. Instead of honoring the white flag, the Indians said, Chapman immediately raised his rifle and fired twice at the truce team, missing both times. As the Nez Perce quickly withdrew to cover, Theller ordered his trumpeter to sound the battle call, but before Jones could do so, he was killed by a shot from Otstotpoo (Fire Body), one of the warriors hidden on the troops' flank.

As Perry saw his advance guard come under fire, he ordered his men into line to begin a charge. Meanwhile, volunteers led by George Shearer, a former Confederate officer, galloped ahead on their own to attack the Indian camp, but Indian fire sent them reeling back to a defensive position on a knoll on Perry's left flank. At the same time, Perry had troubles of his own. Both of his other two trumpeters had lost their instruments, and Perry had difficulty communicating his orders. He got F Company to the crest of a ridge, which he decided to hold rather than attempt an attack that would only drive the Nez Perce into the dense brush cover along White Bird Creek. As H Company moved up to occupy the right side of the ridge, both sides of Perry's line were struck by the Nez Perce who had been hiding behind hills on the flanks. From the right, ʔalok̓at and a large group of warriors, including Wahlitits, Sá·psɪs ʔɪlp̓ílp, and a friend named Tipyalahnah Kapskaps, all flaunting their courage by wearing red blanket coats that made them good targets, charged into and around H Company, frightening the horses and disorganizing the men. At the same time, another group of Nez Perce, including Yellow Wolf and Two Moons, swept from behind some small hills on the left and quickly scattered the volunteers from the knoll, exposing Perry's whole line. With Indians all about them, the troopers were soon pushed backward. Though the cavalrymen fought bravely, the continued Nez Perce pressure forced a general retreat, which gradually became a rout. Without a trumpeter, Perry had to gallop from one group to another, yelling to his men to hold. It was no use. The units broke into fragments, some of the men on foot, others on horseback, and all of them trying to get back up the long slope or climb the bluffs along the steep western wall of the canyon. Seven men under

Theller were trapped in a brush-filled ravine and killed. Again and again, Perry chose positions from which to make a stand, but each time the Nez Perce panicked his men into flight.

As the command disintegrated, the Indians chased the fleeing troopers all the way up the canyon and to within six kilometers (four miles) of Mount Idaho, where they finally abandoned the battle and returned to their camp. On the way up the slope, the Indians had captured three reservation Nez Perce. They took them back to their village, scolded them, and let them go with a warning that if they helped the soldiers again and were caught, they would be whipped. The beaten troops and volunteers, meanwhile, withdrew to Grangeville, and Perry sent a messenger to Lapwai with news of his disastrous defeat. On the battlefield lay Theller and thirty-three enlisted men, dead, a third of his command; he had previously left several men at Grangeville and had gone into battle with ninety-nine troopers. The Indians had only three men wounded, one of whom was cut by a rock during a fall, and none killed. At the same time, the Nez Perce retrieved from the battlefield sixty-three army rifles and a large number of pistols.

The news of what was immediately called another Indian "massacre," though it was not as catastrophic as the one suffered almost exactly a year before by Custer, stunned Howard and roused the nation with a demand that he do something about it. Though the non-treaty Nez Perce had wanted to make peace and be left alone, the whites viewed them as hostiles who had deliberately started a new war. Their ignominious drubbing of the army made front-page headlines, and the Nez Perce tribe and its presumed "renegade" war leader, Chief Joseph (who had fought, but not led, at White Bird), were suddenly household names. War correspondents and magazine illustrators flocked to Idaho to cover the pursuit of the non-treaties, whom Howard promised would soon be captured and punished.

At the same time many whites began watching Indians throughout Idaho and in eastern Washington and Oregon for signs that they might join Chief Joseph and panicked at reports of threats and rumors of strange movements. On the Nez Perce reservation fear and excitement were heightened by constant alarms that Joseph and the hostiles were about to attack the reservation and the Lewiston area, and treaty Indians and whites alike, including ranchers, miners, the missionaries at Kamiah, and Lewiston residents, hurried to Fort Lapwai and the agency for protection. Amid the tension, white anger and prejudice increased against the reservation Nez Perce, and those Indians argued among themselves over the degree of their loyalty. Many Nez Perce families were truly torn, for they had relatives and friends among the warring bands. Even the Christian Indian leaders like the heads of the Reuben and Lawyer families who helped Howard felt sorry for the non-treaties. Some did little to hide their sympathies, and in time a few joined them. But most Protestant Nez Perce did everything possible to display their loyalty to the Americans, and some even charged Catholic Nez Perce with secretly favoring, or helping, the non-treaties.

It took time for Howard to assemble and field a new army, but on June 22 he finally left Fort Lapwai with a punitive force of 227 regulars of the 1st Cavalry, the 21st Infantry, and the 4th Artillery, together with packers, guides, two Gatling guns, a mountain howitzer, and a company of twenty civilian volunteers from Walla Walla. Meanwhile the non-treaties were joined at White Bird Creek by a group of Nez Perce, including two of the tribe's most respected war leaders, Wacámyos (Rainbow) and Pá·qatas ʔewyí·n (Five Wounds), who had been buffalo hunting in Montana. Knowing that Howard's soldiers would again come looking for them, the chiefs directed a group of warriors to return to Tıpaʔxlíwam to watch the Camas Prairie for troops. Then the bands moved up the Salmon to Horseshoe Bend, crossed the river on June 19, and climbed to the high country between the Salmon and the Snake. Howard lingered on the White Bird battlefield to bury the dead cavalrymen and did not reach the Salmon crossing until June 27. That day he received reinforcements of 175 regulars and, soon afterward, a group of volunteers from Dayton, Washington, who relieved the Walla Walla unit.

Though his men were taunted from across the river by non-treaty rearguard scouts, who eventually rode off to join their people in the mountains, Howard was not able to start crossing the Salmon until July 1. By that time, he was in trouble. On June 29, he had received reports that Looking Glass's reservation band at Clear Creek on the Middle Fork of the Clearwater, far to his rear, was recruiting warriors for Joseph and showing signs of joining the non-treaties. The reports had been false and seem to have originated among the Mount Idaho settlers, but, on their strength, Howard sent Capt. Stephen Whipple and two companies of cavalry to arrest Looking Glass and end the supposed threat. Whipple had picked up some trigger-happy volunteers at Mount Idaho, and on the morning of July 1 charged savagely into Looking Glass's unsuspecting village, killing and wounding a few people and scattering the rest into hiding. They looted and destroyed the village, made off with many Indian horses, but failed to arrest Looking Glass. Up to then, both Looking Glass and his anti-treaty reservation neighbor, Kulkulsní·nin̈ (Red Owl), had genuinely counseled peace. Now both of them, infuriated by the Americans' treachery, threw in with the warring bands, adding some forty fighting men. Moreover, they now constituted a second force, threatening the Camas Prairie to Howard's rear.

The threat soon became serious. Despite their large number of non-combatants and the big herds of cattle and horses that they drove along with them, the non-treaties whom Howard was pursuing stayed so far ahead of him that on July 2, the day his troops completed their crossing of the Salmon, the Indians re-crossed it far to the north, at the Craig Billy Crossing near Craig's Ferry and the mouth of Captain Billy Creek, getting between Howard and Lewiston and increasing the threat to the Camas Prairie. It took Howard and his column, floundering along the high mountainous trail with their guns and supply train, three more days to reach Craig Billy Crossing, and then they could not get across the turbulent river. Desperate, Howard led his army all the way back to the White Bird Crossing. It was July 8 before his downhearted troops reappeared at their starting point, Grangeville.

The general was greeted with scorn for having let the Indians escape, though he partly offset criticism by lauding what he thought were the brilliant military tactics by Joseph. It was the beginning of a legend that would ultimately characterize the Wallowa chieftain as an "Indian Napoleon." Throughout the hostilities, the whites had no way of knowing that the non-treaty bands were led by their own chiefs and that group councils of the chiefs and war leaders devised common strategy as they went along. As the leader of the Wallowa band, Joseph participated in those councils, but he had no more voice than the others and was sometimes outvoted. ʔalokat, in fact, was the principal tactician and war leader of the Wallowa band, and at times, he, Joseph, and the other chiefs accepted the strategy and advice of the leader of another band, such as Looking Glass. But Joseph's stature as a non-treaty spokesman and diplomat had loomed so large before the war that Howard and the newspaper writers with him readily assumed that he was leading the non-treaties and was responsible for such shrewd tactics as those that had just led the army on a difficult and fruitless chase. As the non-treaties continued to outmaneuver and frustrate the army, the assumption became firmer, and Joseph's reputation as a military genius grew, until the entire conflict became known, undeservedly as it was, as Chief Joseph's War.

The Indians, meanwhile, reappeared on the Camas Prairie. On July 3, the day after the non-treaties re-crossed the Salmon at the Craig Billy Crossing, two citizen scouts came on their advance elements at Craig's Mountain. The Indians unhorsed and killed one of the whites. But the other one raced back to Whipple's command, which had dug in at B. B. Norton's ranch at Cottonwood House, a combination tavern and stage stop, to keep watch over the prairie and wait for Captain Perry, whom Howard had sent back to Lapwai for more ammunition and supplies. Whipple at once dispatched Lt. Sevier M. Rains with ten cavalrymen and two citizen guides to ascertain the Indians' strength. The detachment was ambushed by a party of warriors, including Rainbow, Five Wounds, and Two Moons, and after a desperate firefight, was entirely wiped out. Shortly afterward, Whipple, at the head of his whole command, reconnoitered the area, sighting so many Nez Perce on the mountain that he dared not risk a battle. Aware that the non-treaties had re-crossed the Salmon, he sent messengers to Howard and withdrew to his rifle pits and defenses at Cottonwood.

That night a messenger arrived with word that Perry's pack train was on its way there from Lapwai. Fearing that Perry's group would be attacked, Whipple led his command down the road the next morning and escorted the train to Cottonwood, where Perry, as senior officer, took command. At the same time, Chapman, Shearer, and four other volunteers from Grangeville, having heard of Rains's defeat, arrived and saw how bad the situation was. They got there just in time. By midday, warriors appeared and soon had the whites surrounded. The siege lasted all afternoon, but despite a desultory exchange of fire, there were no casualties on either side, and the Indians finally returned to their camp.

The next day the non-treaty bands began to move eastward across the prairie toward the South Fork of the Clearwater River, passing between Grangeville and the troops at Cottonwood. To shield the non-combatants and livestock as they hurried across the exposed country, the chiefs sent out an advance group of warriors with orders to pin down the troops at Cottonwood and screen the bands. The war party first sighted and chased the two mounted messengers whom Howard was now sending back to Whipple with word that he was dispatching reinforcements to Cottonwood. The Indians failed to run down the couriers, and they reached Perry's rifle pits safely. Seventeen citizen volunteers under D. B. Randall, who had participated in the attack on Looking Glass's camp and who were riding from Mount Idaho to help the soldiers at Cottonwood, were not as fortunate. Randall's men saw the Indians drawn up across their route and tried to charge directly through them and gallop to Cottonwood. The Indians veered aside to let them through, then closed in on them and forced them to run for a place to make a stand. The Indians kept them pinned down until mid-afternoon, killing Randall and another volunteer, wounding three others, one mortally, and suffering two wounded of their own, one of whom died that evening.

Watching from Cottonwood, about 2.5 kilometers (1.5 miles) away, Perry at first refused to risk another White Bird disaster and endanger the supplies he was bringing to Howard by going to the rescue of the beleaguered volunteers. Finally, after the firing slackened, George Shearer galloped safely to the surrounded men, and shortly afterward, Perry sent Whipple and some of his troopers to bring in the volunteers. By then, the non-treaty bands had safely crossed that section of the prairie, and the warriors withdrew. That evening, some fifty volunteers, under George Hunter and Edward McConville, who had left Howard's command and managed to cross the Salmon River at Rocky Canyon, arrived to reinforce Perry. For his delay in rescuing the volunteers, who were soon known as the Brave Seventeen, Perry earned the contempt of the citizens of Camas Prairie, but he was exonerated by a military Court of Inquiry, which found that he had acted correctly in safeguarding the supplies for Howard.

By the time Howard returned to Grangeville on July 8, the volunteers were embarked on another engagement. Taking Randall's survivors and dead and wounded to Mount Idaho, McConville formed a "regiment" of forty-three members of all the different volunteer units and, disgusted with Howard's slowness and ineptitude, started off after the non-treaty bands. They discovered the Nez Perce camped on the South Fork of the Clearwater at the mouth of Cottonwood Creek, but, recognizing that they were not strong enough to attack the Indians, sent a message to Howard to come quickly.

The non-treaties, meanwhile, had been joined by the bands of Looking Glass, Husis Kute, and Hahtalekin, the last two including non-treaty Palouses and Nez Perce from the lower Snake River. The non-treaties now had about 550 women, children, and old men and more than 200 fighting men. They were now within the reservation's eastern boundary, and in the absence of Howard's troops they visited relatives and friends in Kamiah and other reservation villages, luring a few to join them, losing some who were weary of running and fighting, and arguing with Christian and treaty Nez Perce who accused them of bringing trouble to everyone. On one occasion, some non-treaties forced a group of Christian Indians to ferry them across the Clearwater to a shaman-conducted ceremony. As they returned from that meeting, the non-treaties discovered McConville's volunteers hiding near the Indians' camp on the Clearwater's South Fork.

Driven from their concealment, the volunteers moved farther north along the South Fork and dug in atop a hill, where Nez Perce snipers pinned them down. For most of a day and night, the Indians harassed them, driving off most of their horses and keeping them so on edge with a fear of being overrun that they called the hill Mount Misery. On the second day, another group of volunteers sent by Howard broke through the Indians to join them, and soon afterward, the Nez Perce abandoned the fight. After waiting another day for Howard's army to appear, the volunteers left the hill on July 11 and retreated to Mount Idaho.

Their stand, however, had helped to throw the non-treaties off guard. The Indians thought that if Howard and his soldiers showed up again, it would be to help the volunteers, and when that did not occur, they imagined that Howard must be far off. Howard, in fact, was already close to them. As soon as the general had learned from McConville that the volunteers had located the non-treaties' camp, he had left Grangeville. Instead of marching to relieve McConville's volunteers, however, he had taken a more southerly route, reaching the South Fork of the Clearwater well above the Nez Perce camp and the scene of the fighting at Mount Misery. Crossing the South Fork at Jackson's Bridge, he had gone on another six kilometers (four miles) to Walls, where, on July 10, he was joined by Perry and Whipple from Cottonwood. Howard now had a force of some 440 regulars and more than 100 civilian scouts, packers, and volunteers.

He began his march the next morning, moving north along a high, pine-covered plateau on the east side of the South Fork and hoping to trap the non-treaties between his force and McConville's volunteers. A little after noon, just when the volunteers—not having heard from Howard—were abandoning Mount Misery, the troops sighted the non-treaties' camp strung along the lower ground beneath the bluffs of the plateau and across the river to the left of the army's line of march. Ordering his long column to halt, Howard brought his howitzer and Gatling guns to the rim of the bluff and opened fire. The shots fell harmlessly but galvanized the Indians to action. Seizing rifles and cartridge belts and mounting their horses, warriors streamed across the river and up wooded ravines leading to the plateau. At the same time, the troops, who had been marching at some distance to the right of the bluffs' edge, turned left and started for the crest, preparatory to a charge down the steep slope. A group of warriors, led by Tuhuhulcú·t, were too quick for them. Gaining the high ground, they dismounted and, running among the trees and rocks, got between the troops and the crest, halting the soldiers' advance.

Up ahead, other Nez Perce, including ʔalokat, Rainbow, and Five Wounds, scrambled to the high ground and struck Howard's pack train, killing two packers and, for a moment, almost capturing the train. Farther south, still other warriors appeared, threatening Howard's rear elements. The ferocity of the Indians' attack forced Howard to pull his units together on a small, open tableland. As the Indians formed a semicircle around him, firing at his men from the fringes of trees along the crest and in ravines on the north and south, he established a long, elliptical defense. The battle raged throughout the day, with neither side able to dislodge the other. The troops dug in with trowel bayonets and lay prone behind rocks, while the Nez Perce tried to pick them off. The lines, however, were widely separated, and the firing was generally ineffective. Howard tried several times to launch attacks, and with the help of his howitzer succeeded temporarily in driving Nez Perce from small sections of their siege line. But each time the warriors came back, sometimes with sudden bold rushes by individuals or small groups, who lunged close to the troops before dashing back to cover.

It was a broiling hot day, and the soldiers suffered from thirst. They located one spring but could not get to it until after dark. They worried whether they were to share Custer's fate. They dug their holes deeper during the night, stayed on the alert, and exchanged occasional shots with the Indians. In the morning, the Nez Perce were still there. Howard marveled at what he thought was more evidence of Joseph's skillful generalship. The troops had taken the Indian village by surprise, but were now almost surrounded and fighting for their lives. Rarely in Indian warfare, moreover, had warriors displayed the leadership or patience to maintain such a determined siege.

After daylight, Howard tried to break the stalemate. Bringing the howitzer into play, he managed only to drive the Indians from around the spring and secure the water source for his men. Unknown to him, however, dissension was weakening the non-treaties. During the night, many warriors had returned to camp to oversee the welfare of the people and had argued over whether to flee or continue to fight. The arguing became more serious the next morning. An increasing number of warriors questioned the chiefs, insisting that they should protect the people, get them away without losses, and then withdraw from the fight before more lives were sacrificed. Gradually, individuals and groups began to desert the battlefield and ride back to the village.

Howard, meanwhile, was planning a new attempt to break out. He noticed the Indians' fire decreasing but thought little of it, and by 2:30 p.m. he was ready to launch his attack. The arrival of a supply train, escorted by reinforcements and twenty treaty Nez Perce scouts, held him up, but only momentarily. He sent one unit to bring in the newcomers. On its way back, the unit, by prearranged plan, charged suddenly at the Indians' right flank. The Nez Perce fought back but were outflanked. At the same time, Howard ordered a general attack all along the line. To the soldiers' surprise, the weakened Indian forces, after a brief resistance, broke and ran, fleeing down the slope to the village. The exultant troops fired after the retreating Indians, then moved down the ravines to the river. By the time they reached the non-treaty camp, the last of the Indians were disappearing. Sensing that the defections would mean the end of the battle, the chiefs had earlier sent Joseph down the hill to help get the people safely away. Some of them were still gathering their possessions and driving their stock into the hills when the warriors' line crumpled.

Though Howard had had thirteen men killed and twenty-seven wounded, two of them fatally, while the Nez Perce lost only four dead and six wounded, the general thought that he had scored a decisive

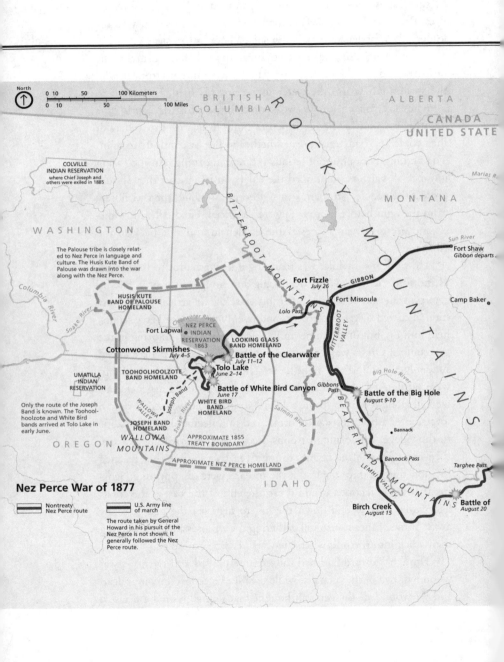

Nez Perce War of 1877

North

0 10 50 100 Kilometers
0 10 50 100 Miles

BRITISH COLUMBIA

ALBERTA

CANADA
UNITED STATE

ROCKY MOUNTAINS

Marias R.

MONTANA

COLVILLE
INDIAN RESERVATION
where Chief Joseph and
others were exiled in 1885

WASHINGTON

Sun River

Fort Shaw
Gibbon departs

BITTERROOT MOUNTAINS

The Palouse tribe is closely related to Nez Perce in language and culture. The Husis Kute Band of Palouse was drawn into the war along with the Nez Perce.

Columbia River

Snake River

HUSIS KUTE
BAND OF PALOUSE
HOMELAND

Fort Fizzle
July 26

GIBBON

Fort Missoula

Camp Baker

Lolo Pass

Clearwater River

Fort Lapwai

NEZ PERCE
INDIAN
RESERVATION
1863

LOOKING GLASS
BAND HOMELAND

BITTERROOT VALLEY

Cottonwood Skirmishes
July 4–5

Battle of the Clearwater
July 11–12

Big Hole River

TOOHOOLHOOLZOTE
BAND HOMELAND

Tolo Lake
June 2–14

Battle of White Bird Canyon
June 17

Gibbons
Pass

Battle of the Big Hole
August 9–10

UMATILLA
INDIAN
RESERVATION

Joseph Band

Snake River

WHITE
BIRD
BAND
HOMELAND

Salmon River

BEAVERHEAD

Bannack

Only the route of the Joseph Band is known. The Toohoolhoolzote and White Bird bands arrived at Tolo Lake in early June.

WALLOWA
VALLEY

JOSEPH BAND
HOMELAND

Bannock Pass

OREGON

WALLOWA
MOUNTAINS

APPROXIMATE 1855
TREATY BOUNDARY

LEMHI VALLEY

MOUNTAINS

Targhee Pass

APPROXIMATE NEZ PERCE HOMELAND

IDAHO

Birch Creek
August 15

Battle of
August 20

Nez Perce War of 1877

Nontreaty
Nez Perce route

U.S. Army line
of march

The route taken by General Howard in his pursuit of the Nez Perce is not shown. It generally followed the Nez Perce route.

Nez Perce Homeland and the 1877 War

Nez Perce (Nee-Me-Poo) National Historic Trail follows the route of the Nez Perce War. The 1,170-mile trail begins at Wallowa Valley, Oregon, travels through Big Hole National Battlefield, and ends at Bear Paw Battlefield, Montana. Several of the Nez Perce War sites are preserved and interpreted by Nez Perce National Historical Park, the U.S. Forest Service, and other agencies.

Courtesy National Park Service, Nez Perce National Historical Park.

This map of Nez Perce Country shows, with the exception of the Lewis and Clark Expedition, the major events of the nineteenth century faced by the Nez Perce. The dashed border shows the extent of the Nez Perce people through all central Idaho to southeastern Washington and northeastern Oregon. The treaty of 1855 set aside almost this entire area as a reservation for the Nez Perce. The discovery of gold just five years later led to a new treaty that was finally ratified in 1867. The reservation established by this treaty is one-tenth the size of the 1855 reservation. The Nez Perce War of 1877 began in the vicinity of Tolo Lake, where Joseph and the non-treaty bands had camped prior to moving onto the reservation. After the initial victory at White Bird, the Nez Perce launched their futile yet heroic flight, hoping to find aid and refuge. The end came three and one-half months later at a place just shy of the Canadian border and Sitting Bull's hospitality. The heavy line shows this historic trek.

victory at what became known as the Battle of the Clearwater. But he now committed a grave error. Instead of ordering an immediate pursuit of the non-treaties and ending the war there and then, he postponed the chase until the next day and permitted his men to swarm through the tipis and help themselves to the many personal possessions and goods that the Nez Perce families had abandoned.

In the intervening time, the non-treaties, viewing their escape as a victory but shaken by their close call and the loss of almost everything they owned, made their way down the Clearwater and gathered near Kamiah. The next morning they made bullboats and crossed the river to the east bank, swimming across the two to three thousand horses they still possessed. Heading toward the Weippe prairie, their main body disappeared in the hills just as Howard's advance cavalry reached the place where they had crossed. A rearguard of warriors skirmished briefly with the cavalrymen and then joined their people when Howard's main command began to appear.

Howard dallied at the crossing for another full day, planning his next move. His treaty Nez Perce scouts, including old Captain John and James Reuben, suggested a way by which Howard could intercept the non-treaties by taking a shortcut to Weippe, but the plan miscarried and cost Howard still another day's delay. The non-treaties, meanwhile, reached the Weippe camas-gathering grounds. On July 15, in a council that seems to have been marked by dissension between Joseph and Looking Glass and mediated by White Bird, the Indians agreed to Looking Glass's proposal that they cross the Lolo Trail and seek sanctuary on the plains with his buffalo-hunting friends, the Crows. There is evidence that Joseph at first opposed traveling away from their homeland and even argued that they go, instead, to the Flatheads. It is also known that the Wallowa leader and members of his band disliked Looking Glass's officious manner. But still other evidence made Howard believe that the Battle of the Clearwater had so disheartened Joseph that he wanted to give up but was restrained from doing so by the other chiefs. Just before the bands reached Weippe, one of Joseph's warrior's, Ta-min Tsi-ya (No

Heart), had appeared on the bank of the Clearwater opposite Howard's troops and had led the general to understand that Joseph wanted
to surrender. It may have been a taunt, however, for the warrior soon
rode away, and nothing came of it.

At any rate, Looking Glass, who was familiar with Montana and
told the other chiefs that the whites there would have no reason to
fight them, was made war leader and guide for all the bands. And on
July 16 the non-treaties began their trek across the Bitterroots. The
next day, Howard, at last, sent a large force from the Clearwater to
find them. The unit tracked the non-treaties to the Lolo Trail, but
when Nez Perce treaty scouts in its lead were ambushed by Rainbow
and other warriors, the troops gave up the pursuit and returned to
Howard. As the non-treaty families and their large horse herd continued their difficult way across the windfall-choked and little-used
mountain trail, the War Department figured out what to do next.
Though the Indians were leaving the military district of Howard's
Department of the Columbia, he was ordered to continue the pursuit. At the same time, troops in Montana were alerted to try to halt
the Nez Perce when they appeared at the eastern end of the Lolo
Trail.

It took Howard almost two weeks to resume his pursuit. After re-
organizing and resupplying his command and arranging for the security of the recent theater of fighting in case the non-treaties doubled
back or other Indians became hostile, he started for the Lolo Trail
on July 30 with 700 men, including Ad Chapman, the Salmon River
volunteer interpreter, and a group of treaty Nez Perce who acted as
guides and horse herders. Aided by a company of axmen from Lewiston who cleared the route, Howard took nine days to cross the mountains. By then, he was far behind the Nez Perce, who had started their
descent of the eastern slope on July 25. The War Department's word
of their movements had preceded them, and a detachment of 35 regulars under Capt. Charles C. Rawn from Missoula, joined by some
Bitterroot Valley settlers and a small group of Flathead Indians, had
erected a log barricade across the eastern end of the trail. After a series

of councils with Rawn and the settlers, the chiefs avoided bloodshed by simply leading the bands up to higher ground and around the barricade, which was thereafter known as Fort Fizzle.

In the Bitterroot Valley, the non-treaties turned south and, without serious opposition from the settlers—some of whom knew Looking Glass and now willingly sold supplies to the Indians—traveled to its head and then over a pass to the Big Hole Valley. Though some people were uneasy, Looking Glass persuaded them that they could take time to rest and cut new lodge poles, and they stopped at an old campsite known as ʔıckuṁkuṁé·lıxpe (Place of Ground Squirrels) at the junction of Trail and Ruby creeks, just below the wooded mountain they had crossed.

It was August 7. Unknown to the Nez Perce, 163 regulars of the 7th Infantry commanded by Col. John Gibbon had reached Missoula from a number of different posts in Montana and were now close by. Joined by thirty-four area volunteers, Gibbon ascended the mountains, located the Nez Perce camp below him in the Big Hole Valley, and prepared to attack it. At dawn on August 9, while most of the Indians were deep in sleep after a night of singing and dancing, Gibbon's men came out of the woods in a skirmish line, shot an elderly Indian who was checking the horse herd, and charged across the stream and into the camp.

In the first confused fighting, many Indians were killed. People awoke with a start and were shot, clubbed, and cut down as they tried to flee. Others managed to grab weapons and fight back, sometimes hand-to-hand. As the women and children raced to get away, groups of warriors finally stalled the attack. On the left and in the center, savage fighting swirled among the tipis. On the right, Gibbon's principal junior officer was killed, and the leaderless regulars and volunteers faltered. The swift Indian recovery slowly pushed the troops toward the center, where some of the soldiers were trying to set fire to the tipi covers. They were tough and wet with frost, but finally some went up in smoke and flames and added to the confusion.

Amid the tumult, the chiefs urged on the warriors to drive the soldiers from the camp. Indians who had run from the village during the first attack began to move back, picking off individual soldiers from their places of concealment. Others joined groups at each end of the camp and caught the troops in a crossfire. Gibbon was hit in the thigh, and several of his officers went down, killed or wounded. The troops gradually lost all sense of order. Fearing an Indian counterattack that would overwhelm them, Gibbon ordered a withdrawal to an elevated bench among the trees at the base of the mountain. Carrying their wounded, the regulars and volunteers fought their way to the position, where they formed a square defense and dug in behind logs and boulders. As the Nez Perce swarmed after them, the battle suddenly reversed itself. The warriors quickly built up a firing line around the troops, and another siege began.

The village, meanwhile, was the scene of anguish. Numerous women, children, old people, and warriors, including Rainbow, Wahlitits, and the Palouse leader, Hahtalekin, lay slain, and many more were seriously wounded, including the wives of Joseph and ?alokat. There was little time to grieve, however. Once more, while the warriors kept the troops surrounded, the people had to get away. With Joseph supervising their preparations, the women and some men hastily scooped burial places for the dead, placed the badly wounded on travois, and struck the camp. At noon Joseph and White Bird hurried the column of mourning families and the horse herd off toward the south.

On the wooded hill, the warriors maintained their siege throughout the day. Both sides suffered casualties. Among the Indian losses were Five Wounds and Sá·psis ?ɪlp̓ɪ́lp. At one point, a number of warriors rode up the mountain trail to intercept a howitzer train and ammunition mule, which Gibbon had ordered to join him after his dawn attack. The Indians killed one member of the detail, wounded another, chased the rest away, and captured the train. They dismantled the howitzer and distributed the ammunition to the Nez Perce at the siege line.

At nightfall, many of the Indians broke off the siege and hurried after the families. ?alokat and a dozen of the younger men remained behind, keeping the troops pinned down and listening in the darkness to the groans and cries of Gibbon's wounded men. At day-break, the Indians departed. Gibbon was in no condition to follow them. Twenty-nine soldiers and volunteers were dead and forty were wounded, two of them mortally. The next day, Howard and some of his troops reached the scene, having finally crossed the Lolo Trail and come up the Bitterroot Valley. Howard again took command of the pursuit and, leaving doctors with Gibbon's survivors, who would return to their Montana bases, set out again after the Nez Perce.

Though the non-treaties had once more escaped, the surprise at-tack at the Big Hole had dealt them a serious blow. Between sixty and ninety of their people, including many women and children and twelve of their best warriors, had been killed. Every family felt a loss. They were angry with Looking Glass, who had promised them safety in Montana and had lulled them into believing that there was no danger in resting at the Big Hole, but they were more bitter at the whites who had wantonly killed their women, children, and old peo-ple. Though Joseph and the other chiefs advised against blind hate, they had trouble thereafter controlling the angry younger men, who decided that they would now treat all whites, civilians as well as sol-diers, as enemies.

Disillusioned by Looking Glass, the chiefs selected a new guide, a mixed-blood Nez Perce named Wewúkıye wısé·w (Lean Elk). He had spent much of his time in Montana, where many of the whites knew him as Poker Joe, and was familiar with the route to the Crows. Starting off again, the non-treaties then crossed Horse Prairie and Bannock Pass and, reentering Idaho, turned east toward the newly created (in 1872) Yellowstone National Park. Along the way, many of their wounded died and were buried, and some young warriors ig-nored the chiefs' attempts to restrain them and raided ranches, drove off horses, and killed a number of whites. Coming on after them, Howard found the whole countryside alarmed and taking to stock-ades. He increased his pace and, after failing to intercept the Indians as they moved eastward toward the park, almost overtook them. On August 20, at Camas Meadows just west of the park, he was set back, however, when a party of warriors, led by ʔalokat, Looking Glass, and Tuhuhulcú·t, ran off his mule herd during the night, immobilizing his train of supplies and ammunition. He sent mounted troops in pursuit, but after a sharp fight, the Indians got away with most of the mules. Once more Howard fell behind.

On August 21 the Indians entered the park at present-day West Yellowstone and, moving up the Madison and Firehole rivers and present-day Nez Perce Creek, crossed the high, wooded central plateau to Hayden Valley. The chase through the park made sensational headlines throughout the nation. Lean Elk was not sure of the route to Hayden Valley, and the bands captured a prospector who agreed to guide them. Soon afterward, Yellow Wolf and several other Indians scooped up a party of nine tourists. Fearing that they would tell Howard of their whereabouts, the bands carried the frightened tourists along with them. After several escaped and two were wounded and abandoned, the others were set free near Hayden Valley. The bands then ascended Pelican Creek and, via Lamar River and Cache Creek, threaded through the high Absaroka Range to the Clark Fork River that ran down to the Yellowstone River on the plains. As a rearguard, they left behind three small parties of warriors, who ran into more tourists, killed and wounded several of them, burned a ranch, and captured some horses before riding to join the bands.

Though Howard, with a reequipped column, was far behind, other forces had been hurried to the northern and eastern sides of the park to try to trap the Indians. Directed by Gen. William Tecumseh Sherman, the commanding general of the U.S. Army who had toured the park just before the Nez Perce had entered it, Col. Samuel D. Sturgis, with six companies of Custer's old command, the Seventh Cavalry, went to block the Clark Fork River exit. Five companies of the 5th Cavalry and 100 scouts were stationed at the Shoshone River exit, near present-day Cody, Wyoming, in case the Nez Perce used that route. Despite the trap, the non-treaties got through. Though events are unclear, it appears that the Indians fooled Sturgis's scouts into believing that they had abandoned the Clark Fork route because of the narrowness of its canyon and were, instead, coming down the Shoshone. Hurrying to that river, Sturgis moved up it, only to discover that the non-treaties were already well down the Clark Fork. Moreover, Howard, still pursuing the Indians, had also started down the Clark Fork and was ahead of him.

Sturgis caught up with Howard on the lower part of the river, and the chagrined officers, now 80 kilometers (50 miles) behind the Indians, sent couriers to Col. Nelson A. Miles at Fort Keogh near present-day Miles City urging him to cut northwestwardly across Montana with his troops and intercept the Nez Perce. Meanwhile, Sturgis, with more than 400 cavalrymen, took out ahead of Howard to continue the pursuit. On September 13, he overtook the Nez Perce at Canyon Creek, on the northern side of the Yellowstone, west of present-day Billings. While the bands hurried northward toward the safety of a narrow canyon, the warriors fired from behind rocks and the cover of washes to hold off the troops. Their success finally induced Sturgis to order his men to dismount and advance on foot in a skirmish line. It was an error that let the bands reach the canyon and disappear from sight. Slowly, the warriors withdrew, but their fire from the rims of the canyon continued to harass the troopers until dusk, when Sturgis called off the pursuit until the next day. In the skirmishing, he had three men killed and eleven wounded, while the Nez Perce suffered three wounded.

The non-treaties had escaped again, but as they hastened north, out of the canyon and onto the plains, they were harried, unexpectedly, by a new enemy. Bannock Indian scouts from Idaho, who had been with Howard, had combined with a unit of Crow scouts, accompanying Sturgis, and they now overtook the Nez Perce, darting at the rear and flanks of the moving column, killing stragglers, stealing horses, and engaging in brief, running skirmishes with Nez Perce warriors. The non-treaties finally drove them away, but the hostility of the Crows, who they had once thought would welcome and help them, was another disillusionment. Now, the chiefs, recognizing the growing weariness of the people after all their suffering and trials, decided that their only salvation lay in reaching the Canadian border and joining Sitting Bull, whose Hunkpapa Sioux had been interred but given safety in Canada after the Battle of the Little Bighorn.

Crossing the Musselshell River, they passed through the Judith Basin, and on September 23 reached the Missouri River opposite a steamboat freight depot at Cow Island Landing. After a brief skirmish with some soldiers and civilians guarding the depot, the Indians helped themselves to some much-needed food and supplies among the freight and continued on toward Canada, skirmishing again with some freighters and driving off another unit of troops from Fort Benton. On September 29, after passing the main range of the Bear Paw Mountains, they reached Snake Creek that ran north to the Milk River. They were less than 65 kilometers (40 miles) from the Canadian border.

An arctic wind, with a hint of snow, whipped across the barren, almost treeless plains. The people were tired, hungry, and cold, and Looking Glass, who had again assumed leadership, persuaded the other chiefs to let the bands rest until the next morning. A camp was established in the shelter of a crescent-shaped depression along the creek, cut by a network of deeper coulees and ravines and protected by low bluffs and rocky ridges. Hunters brought in some buffalo meat, and the different bands built buffalo-chip fires in the coulees and settled down to eat and sleep.

It was to be their last camp. On September 18, Miles had left Fort Keogh with 383 men of the 2nd and 7th Cavalry and the 5th Infantry, a company of Cheyenne and Sioux scouts, a Hotchkiss gun, and a Napoleon cannon, and had hurried across the Missouri River toward the Bear Paw Mountains. North of that range, he had turned west, approaching the area where the non-treaties were resting. At six in the morning of September 30 his Cheyenne scouts discovered the Nez Perce camp, and two hours later Miles's cavalry attacked.

The bands had received just enough warning from their own sentries to prepare for the onslaught. As some of the people ran for their horses, warriors climbed the cutbanks and slopes and scrambled behind rocks and into depressions. They waited until the cavalrymen were 180 meters (200 yards) away, then opened fire, shattering the troopers' ranks. As the charge collapsed, the Indians and cavalry-men, many of them unhorsed and wounded, fought briefly at close quarters. The dazed troopers finally turned and raced from the Indians' fire, leaving sixteen men dead. In all, fifty-three officers and enlisted men were killed or wounded. One wing, however, had success. Swinging left, it circled to the rear of the camp and crashed into the Indians' pony herd, scattering the Indians there and driving off most of the Nez Perce mounts. Many of the Indians fled across the country, and members of the unit went on and captured those whom they overtook.

Miles followed his first charge with a second and then a third. Both were thrown back with heavy casualties, though the last one carried some of the troopers over the rim and into the camp of Joseph's band, where the soldiers fought hand-to-hand with the Wallowa chief and his people before they were forced out again. Even Miles's Hotchkiss gun, which had been rushed to a ridge northwest of the village, was temporarily abandoned when its detail was sent running by Nez Perce sharpshooters.

In the face of fierce Indian resistance, Miles finally called off the costly attacks and established a siege line around the camp. The soldiers dug shallow rifle pits, and the battle settled down to an exchange of marksmanship. With the coming of night, the firing slackened, though the Nez Perce stayed on guard. Within the hollow, the people scooped out shelter holes in the walls of the coulees and ravines and took stock of their losses. Among the day's dead—twenty-two men, women, and children—were ʔaloḵat, Tuhuhulcú·t, and Lean Elk. In the darkness a heavy snow began to fall, but there could be no fires. The children cried in the cold.

The siege went on in the bitter weather for five more days, with people dying on both sides and the Indians' suffering growing more intense. In the fighting of the first day a number of Nez Perce had managed to escape the cavalry, and during the following nights more got away safely. Some eventually reached Canada and Sitting Bull's camp, but many died of exposure or hunger or were rounded up by troops or murdered by Indians of other tribes. Those in the camp were unaware of their fate, but they hoped that they had reached Sitting Bull and would persuade him to come to their help. Miles, too, was aware of that threat. But he also wanted to end the battle before Howard arrived to take from him the credit for the non-treaties' surrender. He made several anxious efforts to parley with Joseph, and at length, under a white flag, succeeded in arranging a meeting at which he promised the Wallowa chief that if the Nez Perce surrendered, they would be detained at Fort Keogh only during the winter and could then return to their own country. When Joseph declined the offer, Miles held him for a while as a prisoner, then exchanged him for an officer whom the Nez Perce had captured.

Meanwhile Howard, accompanied only by two aides, Ad Chapman, two treaty Nez Perce, and a detachment of seventeen men, had pushed on ahead of Sturgis and the rest of the troops and on October 4 arrived at the battlefield. He reassured Miles that the younger man could accept the Indians' surrender and agreed with him that the Indians could be told that they would be returned to their homes. The next morning, they sent the two treaty Nez Perce into the non-treaties' camp to try to persuade them to surrender. The negotiators failed and were sent back to Howard, but in the hollow a council followed among the remaining chiefs and leading warriors, during which Joseph argued for surrender to spare the people further suffering. The two other surviving chiefs, White Bird and Looking Glass, were adamantly opposed to giving up, however, claiming that they would be hanged like the chiefs whom Wright had hanged in the 1850s. Both of them finally told Joseph that he could do what he wished, but that they intended to try to steal off with their people and reach Sitting Bull.

Shortly afterward someone called that a mounted Indian was approaching from the north. It was one of Miles's Cheyennes, but thinking it was a messenger from Sitting Bull, Looking Glass sprang up to see for himself and was instantly killed by a shot that tore away the top of his head.

That afternoon, Joseph surrendered. There are various versions of how he did it. According to one of them, he had earlier sent his famous surrender message to Howard via the treaty Nez Perce when they had left the non-treaties' camp in the morning and then, about four in the afternoon, simply rode out, accompanied by five of his warriors on foot, and from horseback offered his rifle, first to Howard, then to Miles. This account would imply that Ad Chapman, in the morning, translated words that the treaty Nez Perce carried from Joseph.

According to the better-known account, Joseph rode up from his camp in the coulees accompanied by the five men about 4 p.m., dismounted, and offered his rifle to Howard. Howard motioned him to give it to Miles, who was to accept the surrender. Then, to Ad Chapman, Howard's interpreter, and with Howard's aide, Lt. C.E.S. Wood, taking down the translated sentences, Joseph spoke his words of surrender:

> Tell General Howard I know his heart. What he told me before, I have it in my heart. I am tired of fighting. Our chiefs are killed. Looking Glass is dead. Tuhuhulcú·t is dead. The old men are all dead. It is the young men who say, yes or no. He who led the young men [ʔalokat] is dead. It is cold, and we have no blankets. The little children are freezing to death. My people, some of them, have run away to the hills, and have no blankets, no food. No one knows where they are— perhaps freezing to death. I want to have time to look for my children, and see how many of them I can find. Maybe I shall find them among the dead. Hear me, my chiefs! I am tired. My heart is sick and sad. From where the sun now stands I will fight no more forever.

It was over. But the heroic, fighting retreat of more than 2,415 kilometers (1,500 miles) by the non-treaty bands was already viewed by the military and the public as an epic of Indian warfare. Some 750 Nez Perce, including women, children, and sick and old people, had stood off a total of more than 2,000 regulars and volunteers of many different army and civilian units, together with their Indian auxiliaries of different tribes, in eighteen engagements, including four major battles and at least four fiercely fought skirmishes. They had lost approximately 65 men and 55 women and children, and had killed approximately 180 whites and wounded 150. For weeks their courage, tenacity, and skill at evading capture had had many of the American people and much of the press sympathizing with their plight and rooting for them. Now, Joseph's surrender speech, when it reached the papers, touched the country's heart.

During the night after the surrender, White Bird and most of his people, together with groups from other bands, stole out of the ravines and started north for Sitting Bull's camp. Though some perished on the way, many made it successfully and found shelter among the Sioux, who claimed that they had been preparing to go to the rescue of the Nez Perce. The remaining non-treaties, 87 men, 184 women, and 147 children, were taken to Fort Keogh, then, despite the promises made to Joseph by Miles and Howard, were dispatched to a camp near Fort Leavenworth, Kansas, where they were held as prisoners of war. The area was a malarial pesthole, and during their confinement most of them became sick and more than twenty-one died. In July 1878 they were moved again, this time by train to Baxter Springs, Kansas, and then by wagons under Indian Bureau jurisdiction to a tract of sand and sagebrush in the northeastern corner of the Indian Territory. There, in a barren and unhealthy country, near present-day Miami in northeastern Oklahoma close to the Missouri border, which they called ʔí·qıspa (The Hot Place), longing for their homeland and still dying from bad sanitation and lack of medicines, they began a period of exile, further punishment for having resisted eviction from lands they had never sold.

Chapter Eight
Aftermath

During the sad years of exile, Joseph never ceased trying to persuade the government to allow the non-treaties to return to their homeland. In the fall of 1878 Commissioner of Indian Affairs E. A. Hayt visited the Nez Perce camp and saw their deplorable living conditions but agreed only to try to get Congress to appropriate money to move them to a different location in the Indian Territory. This was not good enough for Joseph; his people were dying of broken hearts as well as from their unhealthy situation in flimsy canvas tipis that provided little protection against cold and rain. When he told Hayt of the promise that Howard and Miles had made to him at the Bear Paws to return the Nez Perce to the Northwest, Hayt urged the Secretary of the Interior to see if the government had broken the military leaders' word. Both officers confirmed Joseph's story, though Howard maintained that White Bird's flight to Canada had voided the battlefield agreement. Miles disagreed: "I would have started them west immediately [after the surrender] except for the lateness of the season," he asserted. "From all I can learn, the Nez Perce trouble was caused by the rascality of their Agent, and the encroachment of the whites, and have regarded their treatment as unusually severe."

In succeeding months Joseph made similar appeals to every official who visited the Nez Perce, finally inducing the Indian Bureau's inspector general, James O'Neil, to permit him to travel to Washington DC to seek a hearing from President Rutherford B. Hayes. Accompanied by Yellow Bull and Ad Chapman, whom the government—with little regard for the Indians' feeling against him—had hired as interpreter for the exiles, Joseph journeyed to the national capital in January 1879 to see the president, the secretary of the Interior, and other officials. On January 14 he addressed a large assemblage of American and foreign dignitaries who came to see the famous Indian "Napoleon." Instead of hearing a military genius they were stirred by the eloquence of a peace-seeking humanitarian and statesman. In words that were translated by Chapman and later edited for publication in the *North American Review,* Joseph recounted the wrongs done to his people and ended with a moving plea for justice: "You might as well expect the rivers to run backward as that any man who was born free should be contented penned up and denied liberty," he said. "I know that my race must change. We cannot hold our own with the white men as we are. We only ask an even chance to live as other men live. We ask to be recognized as men. We ask that the same law shall work alike on all men. . . . Let me be a free man—free to travel, free to stop, free to work, free to trade where I choose, free to choose my own teachers, free to follow the religion of my fathers, free to think and talk and act for myself—and I will obey every law, or submit to the penalty."

Joseph's speech aroused widespread sympathy but his mission failed. Too many whites in Idaho were still filled with a desire for revenge against the non-treaties, and the government decided it was unsafe to send them back to their homeland. Joseph and his party returned to the Indian Territory, and in June 1879 the Indian Bureau moved the exiles to a more arable and slightly healthier location on the Ponca Indian reserve along the Chikaskia River west of present-day Ponca City, Oklahoma. Still, the people continued to die, some by suicide. "I forgot to tell you in my last about one of the Nez Perce, John Bull," wrote the son of the local Indian agent, Thomas J. Jordan, to his mother in August 1881. "He was very homesick for Idaho and went out where they were digging the grave of one of his friends and shot himself in the stomach . . . he died the next day. He was a full blooded Nez Perce and is the third who has committed suicide. They are all unhappy, discontented and homesick. . . . John Bull said all his friends were dying—that the government only kept them here so that the climate would kill them—so he thought he might as well anticipate matters a little."

In Canada the Nez Perce who had gained safety with Sitting Bull were homesick. Beginning in 1878, individuals and small groups tried to make their way back across the plains and mountains to the Nez Perce reservation. Some died or were killed along the way, and most of those, including Yellow Wolf, who made it safely to Idaho were rounded up on the reservation and sent off under guard to join the exiles in the Indian Territory. White Bird himself never returned; about 1882 his services as a shaman failed to save the lives of two sick Nez Perce children in Canada and he, it is believed, was slain by their distraught father.

In 1879 the government encouraged three young Nez Perce Presbyterian leaders, James Reuben, Mark Williams, and Archie Lawyer, the son of the late head chief, to travel from the reservation to the Indian Territory to teach and preach to the exiles. Williams soon sickened and returned to Idaho, but by February 1880 Lawyer had organized a Presbyterian church among the exiles and Reuben had opened a day school with an average attendance of eighty. In time, a frame schoolhouse was built, and some of the abler students were sent on to an industrial school at the Ponca agency or to the Chilocco Indian Boarding School in the Indian Territory near Arkansas City, Kansas.

Despite their unhappiness, some exiles settled down to making the best of their situation. A sawmill was furnished them, and a number of houses were built. After delays, some non-treaties received cows, chickens, pigs, and additional horses and cattle. Crops were sown, doing well in some years, but being destroyed by drought in others. Even in exile, the Indians were not spared conflict with whites. A number of nearby ranchers allowed their cattle to graze on the Indians' land and trample their crops. Some whites rustled their livestock and, although it was illegal to do so, pressured the agent to lease them parts of the Nez Perce' land, for which the Indians frequently received no pay.

By 1882 Joseph's efforts began to have results. His persuasive appeals had stirred consciences among people outside of the government and had inspired many influential organizations and individuals in the East to take up his cause. Newspapermen and others visited the exiles, interviewed Joseph, and kept his case before the public. Joseph's dignity and personal qualities never failed to impress the whites who met him, and the many articles written about him kept letters, telegrams, and appeals flowing into Washington. By 1883, the Nez Perce plight had become a national issue, and in May of that year James Reuben, who had been seeking permission to return some of the exiles to Idaho, was allowed to take twenty-nine of them back to Lapwai. Two were aged men and the rest widows and orphans. The next year Congress finally gave the Secretary of the Interior authority to send all of the remaining exiles back to the Northwest.

The commissioner of Indian Affairs delayed any action because he was concerned that the whites in Idaho would not peaceably accept the return of Joseph and his Wallowa band, whom the Camas Prairie and Salmon River settlers still erroneously held accountable for the killings that had started the war. Finally he decided to send the remaining Wallowa Nez Perce to the Colville reservation in northeastern Washington and permit the rest of the exiles to settle on the Nez Perce reservation in Idaho. At last, on May 22, 1885, 268 Nez Perce, the remainder of all who had surrendered almost eight years before or who had been captured after the war, entrained at Arkansas City. At Wallula, Washington, they were separated. Joseph and 149 others were sent on to the Colville reservation, while 118 continued to Lapwai. Yellow Wolf thought that only those who had agreed to accept Christianity were permitted to go to Lapwai, while the non-Christians went to Colville. Later events showed, however, that many of those who went to Lapwai did not become Christians.

Joseph and his people continued to suffer an unhappy fate. The Colville reservation had been created in 1872 for a number of Salish and other tribes of eastern Washington, some of whom had not been friendly to the Nez Perce. They now objected to having the Nez Perce non-treaties in their midst, and troops had to be called

Joseph meets with an old foe, John Gibbon, in 1889 on the Colville Reservation. General Gibbon had opposed the Nez Perce at the Battle of the Big Hole on August 9, 1877. Courtesy National Anthropological Archives, Smithsonian Institution (neg. no. 43201).

from Fort Spokane before the Wallowa band could be settled along Nespelem Creek on the reservation. Joseph, too, was not pleased, and until 1900 he clung to the hope that this was only another stopping place. Again and again during the rest of his life, he pleaded in vain to be allowed to return to the Wallowa. In 1889 when the allotment of land began on the Lapwai reservation, he and his people could have moved there and received allotments, but he refused. In 1897 he went again to Washington DC to press his appeal. The Indian Bureau said it would investigate the possibility of the Indians returning to their Oregon homeland, but the Indian officials knew the Wallowa settlers would never permit it. Joseph himself made two visits to the valley of his youth, in 1899 and 1900, and though he received a courteous hearing from the whites who had driven him out more than twenty years before, he was told bluntly that he could not come back. Joseph returned sadly to Nespelem and died there on September 21, 1904, while sitting before his tipi fire. The agency doctor reported that he had died of a broken heart. Joseph was buried at Nespelem, and his grave is still there.

Through the years, antagonisms gradually disappeared between the Nez Perce and the older-settled tribes on the Colville reservation. Some descendants of the Wallowa band eventually moved to Lapwai or married members of other tribes, including the Umatillas and Yakamas, and went to live on their reservations. But many still reside in permanent exile on the Colville reservation and participate in running its government and other affairs. Wallowa County in Oregon, where under the treaty of 1855 the Nez Perce still possess hunting and fishing rights, is still filled with memories of its original owners. At the foot of the Wallowa Lake is the grave of Old Joseph, Chief Joseph's father, Tuekakas, who was originally buried by his own people in the fork of the Wallowa and Lostine rivers when he died in 1871. In 1886, whites, who by then owned the property, opened the grave and shamelessly removed the chief's skull as a souvenir. Years later, in 1926, more respectful whites, with the permission of the Nez Perce tribe, transferred the remains of his body to their present, more prominently-situated resting place. Another important site in the county is an unmarked cave near the mouth of Joseph Creek where the younger Joseph was born in 1840.

The exiles who returned to Lapwai were greeted with warmth and sympathy by relatives and friends, and, without serious opposition by the whites in Idaho, settled among the treaty Nez Perce. The reservation by then had become something of a Presbyterian theocracy, ruled by the government agent but greatly influenced in day-to-day affairs by resident missionaries. The national policy toward Indians had now been established as one of assimilating the Indians into white society as quickly as possible. To achieve that goal, agents and missionaries, often aided by the presence of troops, were receiving the support of the Department of the Interior on reservations to stamp out native beliefs and practices, undermine and destroy traditional forms of leadership and government, and hasten the adoption of the white man's culture and civilization.

During and after the war, this drive toward acculturation made great headway among the treaty Nez Perce. The most influential missionaries on the Nez Perce reservation were two spinster sisters, Sue and Kate McBeth. The former had been sent to Lapwai by the Presbyterians as a government-paid teacher in October 1873. Scottish-born, about forty years old, partly crippled and in feeble health, she possessed the spirit of a crusader bent on eliminating every trace of "heathenish" influence among the Nez Perce. When Spalding died in 1874, she moved from Lapwai to Kamiah, taking up his work of educating young men to become Presbyterian leaders for the tribe. During the excitement at the beginning of the war, she fled to Portland, but in the fall of 1877 returned to Lapwai. Because of complaints that she had done church work on government time, she lost her job as schoolteacher, but she continued as a missionary and in 1879, joined by her newly arrived sister, Kate, went back to Kamiah. With great zeal, and little tolerance for traditional Indian customs, the two strong-willed sisters became a driving force for Presbyterianism and acculturation on the reservation, basing their work at two mission schools at Kamiah. One of them was conducted by Sue for men and the other by Kate for women.

The Presbyterians' methods differed from those of the Catholics. At St. Joseph's Mission on the reservation, the priests were generally more tolerant of Indian ways and customs and worked with the traditional headmen, who organized a council and elected a native chief of all Nez Perce Catholics. Though they had no religious authority, the headmen retained their positions of prestige through their membership on the council, which was responsible for carrying out disciplinary and other tasks and such honors as leading the people in holy day observances. In contrast, the Presbyterians, and the McBeths in particular, not only sharpened the cleavage between Christian and non-Christian Nez Perce but created a factionalism among Presbyterian Indians by giving church status and prominence to anyone they favored, even if they came from families that had never possessed leadership positions in the tribe. Since power became increasingly

centered about the church, those who were ordained as native ministers or elders, or received other leading positions in church societies, inevitably weakened the prestige of families of old-time leaders
who were not similarly favored. Some chiefs, sub-chiefs, and shamans, finding their influence waning, intrigued against the native
ministers and church officers, while the latter, sometimes with the
McBeths' support, fought back by searching for and exposing every
sign of "heathenism," real or fancied. In the process, the factionalism
tended to accelerate acculturation with each side trying to become
more white and Christian than the other.

As the agent and the missionary-dominated Presbyterian church
officials asserted more authority, the formal governing role of the
traditional chiefs lessened, and in 1880, when the twenty-five-year
term of the Stevens Treaty of 1855 expired, it finally disintegrated. To
determine what the Indians wanted done about the treaty, the agent,
Charles B. Warner, called together councils of all adult Nez Perce
males in September 1879 and January 1880. At their request, the Federal Government, on July 1, 1880, continued to enforce the principal
provisions of the 1855 and 1863 treaties. The councils themselves were
innovations and set precedents for governing in the future by general
councils of the adult members of the tribes, rather than by councils
of chiefs. But the renewed treaties eliminated payments to a head
chief or sub-chiefs, thereby ending government recognition of those
provisions. Furthermore, the agent, with the approval of the general
council, drew up a new code of laws to deal with minor crimes on the
reservation (major crimes were handled by Federal courts) and, from
the ranks of leading Presbyterian Indians, appointed an agency police
force of five Nez Perce to enforce the code and a three-member court
of Indian judges with the power to try cases and levy fines as punishments. The police and judges also received salaries, thus further
destroying whatever remained of chiefly rule.

In the years immediately prior to the return of the exiles, acculturation proceeded rapidly. Many Nez Perce cut their hair, adopted white men's clothing, moved into houses, acquired white men's

names, saw that their children attended school and learned to write and speak English, advanced their knowledge of agriculture and mechanical skills, and went to church regularly. At the same time, the missionaries and native Presbyterian church leaders were vexed by the continuing presence and influence of the non-Christians, who still relied on shamans and practiced their old beliefs and customs. Much of the McBeths' time was spent in condemning the "heathens" and in trying to keep their own flocks from being lured to the non-Christians' feasts and celebrations, which were accompanied by drumming, dancing, horse-racing, gambling, drinking, and other activities which the missionaries considered pagan, backward, and immoral. The McBeths' ways irritated the agents, who resented their interference in reservation affairs and complained that they could not control the new aristocracies of native church leaders that the missionaries were creating. In 1885, soon after the exiles' return, friction between the McBeths and one of the agents led to a crisis.

To counteract the Indians' annual Fourth of July celebration at Lapwai the McBeths in 1884 instituted a church-run July outing near Kamiah. The agent at the time was Charles Monteith, John's brother. The next year, Monteith appointed one of the newly returned exiles, Tom Hill Jr., chief of the agency police. While the McBeths' picnic was underway that July, Hill and his police arrived to arrest a participant. A fight occurred, an Indian was fatally wounded, and the picnic was broken up. Hill was indicted for murder, but he was defended by Monteith and eventually was acquitted with a verdict of justifiable homicide. The episode caused great unrest between the Presbyterians and non-Christians on the reservation, as well as bitterness between Monteith and the McBeths. The agent finally ordered Sue McBeth off the reservation, and she was forced to move to Mount Idaho. At the same time, the Presbyterians directed Kate McBeth to leave Kamiah and join another missionary at Lapwai. The uproar did not end there. Many of the Christian Nez Perce turned against Monteith, word of the conflict reached Washington, and after several investigations, Monteith was relieved as agent, though he was reappointed briefly in 1888.

Despite their separation, the McBeths continued to have a great impact on the Nez Perce. Many Indians visited Sue at Mount Idaho, still seeking her counsel and help. In 1890 the sisters were disturbed by a schism at the Kamiah church in which part of the congregation turned against the native pastor, Robert Williams, who in 1879 had been the first Nez Perce to be ordained as a minister. Moving across the Clearwater River, the dissenters established the Second Indian Presbyterian Church under another native minister, Archie Lawyer, who had been with the exiles in the Indian Territory. Though the conflict was marked by a variety of charges brought against Williams, it stemmed basically from rivalry between the prestige-conscious families of old-time chiefs and followers of Lawyer, whose father had been the tribe's head chief, and those of Williams and his church officers, whose families were not of chiefly status. For a long time, the two congregations would have nothing to do with each other, and though passions eventually cooled, the strains of the rift continued for many generations.

Before Sue McBeth died in 1893, nine of the sisters' pupils were ordained as Presbyterian ministers. A tenth was ordained in 1894, and others were ordained later. Some became missionaries to other tribes as far away as the Southwest. On the reservation, differences among the native Presbyterians erupted occasionally during the rest of the nineteenth century, and new churches, with native ministers and church officers, came into being as a result of the factionalism. Kate McBeth continued with her mission work, and in 1899 she was joined by her niece, Mary "Mazie" Crawford. Throughout the rest of her life, she worried about the influences of the "heathens," or "wild ones," as she sometimes called them. Toward the end of the century, she noted with dismay that their number was increasing and that many of the Christians were backsliding. It was the beginning of a gradual decline in the religious fervor of the Indians. Though church membership was maintained, and church offices were regarded as permanent and hereditary by most of their holders, attendance at the Presbyterian churches fell off steadily. From time to time in the twentieth century still other churches, including those of Pentecostal sects, were established, and there were brief revivals of Christian activity, as well as new divisions.

Kate McBeth died in 1915, and Mazie Crawford carried on her work until 1932, when the mission at Lapwai was closed. By then, churches of many denominations had come, and some had gone, but the reservation was still composed of Christian and "heathen" elements. Though the latter term has since fallen into disuse, many Nez Perce still regard themselves as basically non-Christian. For years, moreover, both groups held annual summer gatherings that traced their origins to the "heathenish" Fourth of July celebrations and the McBeths' July picnics. One of them was for the enjoyment of old ways and for those who maintained the traditional spiritual beliefs of their ancestors. The other one, still conducted by the Camp Meeting Association of Talmaks, dates from 1897 when the Joint Session of the six then-existing Nez Perce Presbyterian churches organized a summer camp meeting and revival. It was, and is, essentially a religious, educational, and social retreat and today continues to attract many members of the tribe who enjoy the singing, feasting, and visiting, as well as the Christian religious activities.

Other significant changes came to the reservation after the war. By 1886, the Army had withdrawn troops from Fort Lapwai and turned the site over to the Interior Department. That year the agent, George W. Norris, established a Nez Perce boys' boarding school at the old fort and moved his own office there from the site of present-day Spalding. The agency office was returned to its original site by another agent about 1889, but in 1902 it was permanently established at the fort under agent C. T. Stranahan, who also became superintendent of the school, then known as the Fort Lapwai Training School.

In 1887, Congress passed the Dawes General Allotment Act, which was designed to hasten the assimilation of Indians by breaking up reservations into individual family-sized farms. Each Indian adult was to receive up to 65 hectares (160 acres) and each minor child up to 32 hectares (80 acres). The government would hold the allotments in trust for twenty-five years, after which the Indian owner would be granted a patent in fee and thereafter could sell the land. Whatever

Chief Joseph (*center*) meets with Alice Fletcher and her translator, James Stewart, near Kamiah around 1890. Fletcher and her assistant, Jane Gay, spent twenty-nine months surveying the Nez Perce Reservation and assigning allotments to individual members of the tribe. Courtesy Idaho State Historical Society.

reservation land was left over would be declared surplus and offered for sale to whites by the government. The act was initiated by well-meaning white reformers, mostly in the East, who believed that giving each Indian family its own plot of land would break down tribal relationships, end reservations, and hasten the economic and social improvement of the Indians by encouraging them to become industrious farmers. It was also supported, however, by many other whites who saw it as an opportunity to acquire "surplus" Indian lands.

Around the Nez Perce reservation, there were numerous land-hungry persons who waited eagerly for the reservation to be allotted. In 1889, the government sent a special agent, Alice C. Fletcher, an ethnologist who had been associated with Harvard's Peabody Museum of American Archeology and Ethnology, to divide the Nez Perce reservation. Fletcher, an ardent advocate of the Dawes Act, had already carried out allotments among the Omaha and Winnebago Indians. Accompanied by a photographer friend, E. Jane Gay, she spent four summers among the Nez Perce, completing her assignment in 1893.

At first, she found that many Indians were strongly opposed to the allotment plan, fearful of more changes in their way of life and a further loss of their lands. In 1892 she persuaded a council of the adult members of the tribe to choose a nine-member committee representing the reservation's different population centers to help her in her contacts with the people. Headed by Archie Lawyer and dominated by native Presbyterian church leaders, the committee provided another precedent for later forms of tribal self-government. The committee was able to overcome the people's objections and override their fears, and it speeded Fletcher's job to completion. When she was through, she had made 2,009 allotments to the Indians totaling 70,816 hectares (175,026 acres). She also had persuaded a wealthy Pittsburgh friend to purchase additional allotments for each of the Presbyterian churches and the Catholic mission then on the reservation and give the patents to the church governing bodies.

More than 70 percent of the reservation remained unallotted, and many Nez Perce raised new objections to its sale to whites. Nevertheless, on May 1, 1893, Archie Lawyer and other committee members were pressured by three representatives of the Federal Government to cede the "surplus" lands, some 219,294 hectares (542,000 acres), for $1,626,222. Of this, $1 million was to be paid to the tribe in installments over a period of years, and the remainder was to be distributed to the people on a per capita basis as soon as possible after ratification of the sale. The Nez Perce kept approximately 14,555 of the unallotted hectares (34,000 acres) for timber lands, a cemetery, and other tribal needs. It also was agreed that the ceded lands would not be opened to whites until the Indians received the trust patents for their allotments, and, furthermore, that the provisions of all previous treaties, not inconsistent with the new cession, would remain in force.

The Senate ratified the agreement on August 15, 1894, and on November 8, 1895, President Grover Cleveland declared it to be in effect. The trust patents and first payments were distributed to the Nez Perce, and ten days after Cleveland's announcement the unallotted lands were opened to white settlement. As expected, a huge land boom resulted. On the first morning, some two thousand whites poured onto the reservation, and in one week there were 380 filings of claims. The Nez Perce were soon all but overwhelmed, their own holdings surrounded by those of new white neighbors. The reservation had become a boundary line around a checkerboard pattern of adjoining Indian and white private properties.

The adverse impacts of the Dawes Act did not end there. Many Nez Perce took to ranching and farming on their allotments. But numerous others leased their lands to whites and lived on the income, which was often barely enough to keep them alive. Others moved to populated areas of the whites and sought various wage-paying jobs. In 1906 the passage of the Burke Act led to the alienation of still more of the Indians' land. Under its provisions, Indians who were declared competent to handle their own affairs could be granted citizenship and given patents in fee to their lands without waiting twenty-five years. Again, as expected, many Nez Perce were declared competent and, as quickly, were induced to sell their lands to whites. By the mid-1960s individual Nez Perce owned a total of only 23,087 hectares (57,062 acres) on their reservation.

Accompanying the influx of whites on the reservation was the growth of towns. Population increased on the Camas Prairie, and the town of Spalding was laid out at the mouth of Lapwai Creek to receive the prairie's agricultural products and transship them down the Clearwater. When railroads were built on the reservation at the turn of the century, Spalding's brief boom turned to bust, and the town's population dwindled. Altogether, by 1910, some thirty thousand whites lived on the reservation, as against approximately fifteen hundred Nez Perce. Public schools were built for the whites, and shortly after 1900, Nez Perce children began to attend them in such towns as Kamiah and Lapwai. Other Indian children were sent away to the Carlisle Indian School in Pennsylvania and various Bureau of Indian Affairs boarding schools. All these developments had the effect of speeding acculturation. At the schools, Indian children were not permitted to speak their own languages, and nearly everything about their culture and tribal heritage was drummed out of them. On the reservation, the closeness of the whites had the same impact on their elders. Subjected to prejudice and made to feel inferior by their white neighbors, many Nez Perce strove to imitate the whites and to abandon anything that caused them to feel ashamed. In the process, many of the whites' vices, as well as their material traits, were adopted, contributing to a turning away from deeply held religious and moralistic feelings, both Christian and non-Christian. Slowly, the Nez Perce language, arts, skills, dress, legends, and other cultural traits, including respect for shamans and bonds with guardian spirits, were given up, though not entirely forgotten. In the 1970s, when the Nez Perce' interest in their cultural past was revived, much was still remembered by the older people and could be taught to the young.

During World War I a number of young Nez Perce men served in the U.S. armed forces. When they came back, they contrasted the poor economic and social conditions of the reservation Indians with the more affluent life they had observed elsewhere. Their dissatisfaction paralleled that of many others on the reservation who thought that the Nez Perce should not rely so much on the agent and the Federal Government but should have a governing body of their own that could help the people do more for themselves toward improving their standard of living. Their opportunity to do something came in 1922 when the Bureau of Indian Affairs conducted a survey of reservation conditions. After discussions with the agency personnel, a general council of the adult members of the tribe chose a new nine-member committee, headed by James Stewart, with Corbett Lawyer as secretary, to draw up a five-year program to promote the material and moral improvement of the tribe.

The committee did its job well, setting up an organization known as the Nez Perce Indian Home and Farm Association, with chapters

A Nez Perce family poses for a photograph at the beginning of the twentieth century. The use of cradleboards was still prevalent, as this photograph indicates. Courtesy National Park Service, Nez Perce National Historical Park; NEPE-HI-33783.

in fifteen communities on the reservation. It also drafted a five-year plan to deal with such concerns as health, sanitation, home improvement, employment, education, law and order, the farming of one's own land rather than the leasing of it, parental guidance of children, and the control of vices. The Bureau of Indian Affairs approved the plan, and the Nez Perce in general council formally adopted it on January 22, 1923.

The new organization was a success in many ways. Under the leadership of the nine-member committee, community chapters were formed in a cooperative venture to improve conditions. Support was given by non-Indian organizations, and a number of achievements were scored. Equally significant were the initiative and abilities demonstrated by those who participated. Not only was self-confidence heightened, but many Nez Perce were inspired to wish to go further and create a formal leadership and permanent government for the tribe. In 1926 the adult members of the tribe met again in general council and, with the approval of the agency superintendent, named a new nine-member executive committee to draft a tribal constitution. The document provided for the creation of a general council of all adult members of the tribe that would meet each year and elect a nine-member executive body known as the Advisory Council and Business Committee of the Nez Perce Reservation, which would choose its own officers and meet quarterly. The constitution was sent to the Commissioner of Indian Affairs and was approved by him on October 27, 1927.

Though the constitution was a big step forward, it was discovered soon that it was too weak to give the Nez Perce a government effective enough to meet the tribe's needs. The Business Committee, as the council's executive body came to be known, could deal with such matters as land claims and leases, loan applications, timber sales, grazing permits, marriage laws, and sanitation. But it had no direct control over tribal funds, and its activities were subject to the approval or veto of the superintendent and the Indian Bureau, as well as the support of the often-critical general council. As time passed, it was frustrated increasingly by the superintendent, who used it to help him win tribal acceptance of government-imposed programs but disapproved of what it did when it tried independently to cope with reservation needs.

The passage of the Wheeler-Howard Act, known also as the Indian Reorganization Act, in 1934 provided the Nez Perce with an opportunity to increase the powers of their government and acquire more independence. The act ended the allotment policy that had impoverished many tribes through loss of their lands and resources, restored many cultural freedoms and rights that had long been denied to the Indians, and empowered tribes to write constitutions that set up a stronger form of self-government than the one the Nez Perce possessed. One clause, however, provided that each tribe could vote on whether it wished to accept the statute.

Though many Nez Perce wanted to avail themselves of the opportunity for a more effective self-government, the people as a whole voted against acceptance of the act, 252 to 214, on November 17, 1934. There were many reasons for the rejection. The act was long and complicated, and many did not understand it or were confused or misled about its provisions. Some thought they would lose more land or become subject to taxation. Others feared losing government services. The Presbyterians worried that the new religious and cultural freedoms promised by the act would threaten them by legalizing "heathenism," and still other Nez Perce were concerned that the legislation would enable a powerful few to govern the reservation. The superintendent, moreover, had been moved to an office in Moscow, Idaho, and had been put in charge of three other tribes besides the Nez Perce. As a result, he was absent from the reservation and unable to clarify the provisions.

The negative vote not only made it harder for the Business Committee to broaden its self-governing powers but subjected it to more Federal red tape, restrictions, and scrutiny than was experienced by those tribes that accepted the act. By the late 1930s it was clear to a growing number of Nez Perce that a change was needed. The modern-day needs of the reservation, they could see, required an "up-to-date" new tribal government with more independence from the superintendent and the general council and with powers that would permit it to deal in a businesslike fashion with such reservation affairs as land management programs, health and safety, road maintenance, law and order, hunting and fishing regulations, tribal revenues and budgets, economic welfare, and relations with the federal, state, and local governments.

With the help of Archie Phinney, a Nez Perce employed by the Bureau of Indian Affairs, a revised constitution delegating many duties and powers to an executive committee elected by the general council was prepared by the Business Committee in 1940 and submitted to the Commissioner of Indian Affairs for approval. The tribe received no response until January 1942, when it was informed that the document had been lost in Washington. The nation, meanwhile, had entered World War II, and a further attempt to win approval of the new constitution was abandoned.

During the war many Nez Perce served with honor in the armed forces. Others left the reservation to take war jobs in industry throughout the country. The war accelerated two developments that had already begun. Increasingly, Nez Perce were marrying outside the tribe, not only with members of other tribes but with whites, Latin Americans, and blacks. And more Nez Perce than before began to establish permanent homes off the reservation, principally in nearby towns such as Lewiston and Clarkston.

The contrast between on- and off-reservation standards of living was noted by those who returned to the reservation after the war and found poverty and few opportunities. As had occurred after World War I, a move for a new constitution began. In 1945 a subcommittee of the Business Committee working with Archie Phinney, who had become the reservation's superintendent, drew up a new document that gave so much power to a proposed new executive committee that the people turned it down in an election January 3, 1946. Soon afterward, however, there was a change of mind. The nation was in an economy mood, and word circulated that the Bureau of Indian Affairs was going to close its Nez Perce agency. If that happened, the tribe would have to be ready to run its own affairs. Also, many Nez

Perce decided that a strong executive body was needed to press tribal claims through the Indian Claims Commission established in 1946.

Though the Nez Perce agency—now moved back to Fort Lapwai and called the Northern Idaho Indian Agency for the four tribes that it served—was not closed, economies forced the tribe's business committee to take over land-leasing duties and the responsibility for law and order on the reservation. As more functions were thrust upon the committee, pressure built again for reform. Committee members asserted that they could no longer operate conscientiously because they were being forced to accept responsibilities beyond their constitutional authority, so a new subcommittee of three members, again aided by Archie Phinney, drew up a new constitution. This time it was ratified, ninety-three to seventy-seven, by the general council in a secret ballot on April 30, 1948. The next year, opponents got the council to rescind its approval, but the Commissioner of Indian Affairs ruled the new vote invalid because of irregularities, and the tribe at last had a strong executive body, able to manage reservation affairs. The new nine-member group, known as the Nez Perce Tribal Executive Committee or NPTEC, was elected by the same General Council that ratified the constitution. A host of new powers extending its authority over almost every phase of reservation activity, though much was still subject to approval by the Secretary of the Interior, were delegated to NPTEC by the council, which retained for itself the rights to approve and amend constitutions, elect the executive committee members, and hold referendums.

In succeeding years, various opposition groups, including the "Warriors," the Nez Perce Indian Association, and off-reservation Nez Perce, emerged as a result of dissatisfaction with NPTEC or with its decisions and actions on specific issues. The divisions were sometimes serious, causing factionalism and threatening the continued existence of NPTEC and the constitution of 1948. But each time, the council sustained the executive committee, or the committee itself weathered the attacks, and NPTEC has continued until today as an able and effective governing body.

Chapter Nine
Today

Since 1948 a number of dramatic issues have affected the welfare of the Nez Perce. Though some issues have been accompanied by sharp divisions of opinion among the people, most have contributed materially to the tribe.

One area of activity has been the pursuit of claims. The first one began in 1946, when the U.S. Army Corps of Engineers announced plans to build the Dalles dam on the Columbia River, whose backed-up pool would destroy the traditional Indian fisheries at Celilo Falls. Though the Corps promised to pay the affected tribes for their loss, the Corps, as well as the Yakamas and other tribes that had historically fished at that site, tried to exclude the Nez Perce from any reimbursement. They claimed that Celilo Falls had not been one of the Nez Perce "usual and accustomed" fishing sites, a term used in the Stevens treaties of the 1850s to guarantee recognition of a tribe's continued right to fish at a certain place. Until the establishment of their Tribal Executive Committee under the constitution of 1948, the Nez Perce had lacked a strong central governing body to press its claim in a methodical, businesslike way. After 1948, however, NPTEC proved its worth, enlisting the support of attorneys, anthropologists, and other specialists, and sending delegations to Washington DC, to present compelling documentation of Nez Perce use of the fisheries. The Corps finally acknowledged its error, and in November 1956 awarded the Nez Perce $2,800,000 for the loss of their fishing rights.

At the same time, NPTEC pressed, and won, other claims. These were argued before the Indian Claims Commission, which the Federal Government established in 1946 to end all tribal claims of unjust takings of Indian lands and resources in the past by hearing evidence and awarding payments. Once again with the aid of lawyers and technical experts, NPTEC won victories, being awarded on December 31, 1959, $3 million for the loss of royalties on gold taken from reservation lands in 1860–67 and $4,297,000 for inadequate payment for the lands that Lawyer and his followers had sold the Federal Government under the Treaty of 1863. Some fourteen percent of the latter payment was given to the descendants of the Joseph band for the loss of the Wallowa country of Oregon, for which Joseph and his people had never been paid, though they never wanted to sell.

The pursuit of the claims cases required many years of hard work, dedicated purpose, and the investment of tribal funds for lawyers, expert witnesses, and documentation. While much was learned and the tribe gained valuable experience in the legal, technical, government, and communication procedures of white society, NPTEC and those who handled the claims cases often came under criticism for wasting money or for alleged ineptitude by those within the tribe who thought they would never win. After the victories, further divisions arose over the distribution of awards. In the case of the Celilo Falls money, the commissioner of Indian Affairs permitted the distribution of an initial two hundred dollars to each member of the tribe, but only after the preparation of an accurate and up-to-date roll of all tribal members. When that was completed, the rest of the money, amounting to $1,200 apiece, could only be distributed to individuals when they indicated how they would use the funds for a beneficial family purpose. The distribution of the land and gold claims award money was more complicated. The secretary of the Interior ruled that only about one million dollars of the approximate seven million received in the two awards could be divided on a per capita basis, and, again, only when individuals showed how they would use it beneficially for their families. The rest of the money would have to be earmarked by the tribe for capital investments that would benefit the people as a whole.

The distributions took a long time and caused a serious split within the tribe. NPTEC bore the brunt of the criticism. It carried out the procedures of the Department of the Interior, and many of its members wholeheartedly agreed with what they had been directed to do. As a result, they were charged with favoritism and high-handedness, with dictating to the people how they could spend their money, and, finally, with becoming a small, self-perpetuating clique of politically powerful people who were unresponsive and unaccountable to the general tribal membership. In a short time a move got underway to revise the constitution of 1948, return many of NPTEC's powers to the General Council as the only true representative body of all the people, and bring about reforms in both the Council and NPTEC.

Though many of NPTEC's opponents lived on the reservation, the principal opposition came from those who lived off the reservation and wanted all the awards money distributed on a per capita basis. Of the approximate 2,000 Nez Perce at the time, about 950, or 48 percent, lived off the reservation, and many of them saw little benefit to themselves in money spent for tribal capital improvements on the reservation. Beginning in the late 1950s they formed organizations that fought with NPTEC and, in elections, even managed to get some of their members on that governing body. Finally, compromises were agreed upon, and on May 6, 1961, a revised constitution and bylaws were adopted by the tribe. The principal changes related to voting eligibility on the Council and gave that body increased powers over NPTEC, including the right of recall and a greater role in matters dealing with tribal lands, natural resources, benefits, and the administration of legal suits.

Opposition to NPTEC continued, fed by antagonism to the Bureau of Indian Affairs and to any group of their own people who appeared to be in collusion with or prone to carry out the dictates of, the BIA or any other non–Nez Perce body. But the opponents themselves split from time to time, and one of their factions finally sided with NPTEC. Support for the executive group broadened, also, when it provided leadership to the reservation Nez Perce against the federal government's moves to terminate the tribes. That policy, which meant that the government would end all treaties, services, and other relations with the tribes and turn them and their reservations over to the states—with or without the approval of the tribes—had been in the making since the late 1940s but reached a climax in 1953 with the passage of a Concurrent Resolution by Congress announcing the federal legislature's intent to make termination a reality.

The Nez Perce had striven to gain increased independence from the BIA so at some time they could manage and control their destiny. But it was evident that until they reached a more advanced level of economic and social development and could compete on equal terms with white society, they still required Federal observance of treaty-guaranteed rights, including the delivery of essential services, freedom from certain taxes, and enforcement of the government's trust obligation to protect their land and natural resources. NPTEC joined the National Congress of American Indians (NCAI), a nationwide association of American Indian tribes, in August 1955 and thereby added the tribe's voice to the opposition of termination. Many off-reservation Nez Perce, again seeing no benefit to themselves in the continuation of a reservation and hoping for its breakup and a per-capita division of its assets, generally supported termination. But most of those on the reservation fully supported NPTEC's efforts.

The implementation of the termination policy was finally halted in 1958 after it brought disastrous economic and social consequences to several tribes, and to this day NPTEC, with the support of most reservation Nez Perce, has stood guard against signs of its reinstitution. During the 1960s, the emphasis of the federal government shifted to efforts to assist the economic development of reservations. The Nez Perce benefited from programs of the Area Redevelopment Administration and other agencies. The Office of Economic Opportunity made available Community Action programs, Head Start, and Vista. It also encouraged the tribe to propose its own development programs and then made funds available so the tribe could manage and control the programs itself. This was a landmark change in the relations between federal agencies and the tribes, for prior to that, the BIA, the only agency providing programs to Indians, had generally imposed programs and then controlled their administration and funds. After the OEO's breakthrough, an increasing number of government departments and agencies, including the Department of Health, Education and Welfare (the Indian Health Service had been transferred from the BIA to the U.S. Public Health Service of HEW in 1955), the Department of Labor, the Economic Development Administration, and the Department of Housing and Urban Development, all tailored programs according to the needs as the Indians themselves saw them.

The 1960s and 1970s brought numerous other changes. Joining such regional Indian organizations as the Affiliated Tribes of the Northwest, the Northwest Coordinating Council, and the Idaho State Intertribal Council, the Nez Perce took active leadership roles in modern-day reservation affairs, including the upgrading of the education of their children, the enforcement of law and order on the reservation (though Public Law 280, also passed by Congress in 1953, had conferred on states the right to assume the enforcement of law and order on reservations, Idaho had not accepted the option, and it proved a problem for the Nez Perce), and the increasing assertion of self-determination.

In the early 1960s, using some of its claims money, the tribe built modern community center buildings, encompassing recreation facilities, arts and crafts rooms, and tribal offices at Lapwai and Kamiah. Money for educational scholarship, which NPTEC had written into its earliest budgets, was enhanced, and increased numbers of young Nez Perce were encouraged not only to finish high school but to go to college and graduate school. The Nez Perce development programs and more abundant government funds provided a growing number of employment opportunities on the reservation when students finished their education. And NPTEC led the way in encouraging local public schools to be more attuned in teacher training and the use of learning materials to meet the special needs of Nez Perce children.

Similarly, NPTEC provided loans and worked to assist the needy. Better housing and improved health and sanitation were encouraged. And when an Indian allotment was put up for sale, it first had to be offered to the tribe. In that manner the tribe gradually began to rebuild its domain. By 1970 there were still 21,944 hectares (54,237 acres) owned by individual Nez Perce and the tribe owned 13,612 hectares (33,642 acres).

From time to time in recent years, the tribe has considered investing in sources of income for all the people. Such thinking was responsible, in large measure, for the creation of Nez Perce National Historical Park, with its headquarters and interpretive center at Spalding, Idaho, where so much Nez Perce history occurred. Evolving from a number of studies done for the Nez Perce tribe about 1960 to propose ways in which the tribe could benefit economically by establishing a motel-and-museum complex at Spalding, the national park idea quickly seized the imagination of non-Indian friends of the Nez Perce in Lewiston and elsewhere in the Northwest. Under the leadership of William Johnston, who was then the managing editor of the Lewiston *Tribune,* and supported by the tribe and many white organizations, including the Idaho Historical Society and the Lewiston Chamber of Commerce, a plan was presented to the National Park Service for a unique national park. This park, the first of its kind, would be composed of different sites spread across the ancestral Nez Perce Country and held by different owners. On May 15, 1965, Congress authorized the Secretary of the Interior to designate the park, which has been managed since then on a cooperative basis with the Nez Perce Tribe, the State of Idaho, the U.S. Forest Service, the Bureau of Indian Affairs, local governments, and private organizations and landowners. Together, the sites relate the highlights of the culture and history of the Nez Perce and the dramatic past of the region.

The history of the Nez Perce has not ended anymore than the history of the United States has ended. Each year, the people's story continues to unfold, much of it proving that even the history of their yesterdays is still alive. Though change is evident everywhere, many of their ancient ways, including the use of shamans and sweathouses, live on among them, as if they and their country are timeless. In the new day of Indian self-determination, they are proud to be Nez Perce, proud of their culture and history, and proud of their ancestors, who despite their many trials and sufferings, bequeathed to them a homeland and a still-vibrant heritage.

Index